Praise for
FOREVER HEROES

"It's all here. Moments of terror. Days of tedium. Lifelong pride. This was the reality of World War II for the men and women of the Greatest Generation. More than seven decades later, Joyce Winfield's research and storytelling, based on interviews with Nebraskans who served at the home front and on the front lines, paint vivid and personal pictures that transform these neighbors around us into compelling individuals. They survived torpedoed ships and POW camps, turned shrapnel into a tie clasp and nursed the wounded in the jungles of the South Pacific. These are the ordinary people who did extraordinary things."

> — David Hendee
> Omaha World-Herald reporter
> Contributor to *At War. At Home: World War II*
> and *At War. At Home: The Cold War*

"We had the privilege of taking 1,500 Nebraska WWII veterans on seven Honor Flights in 2008-09. Each had a story to tell. *Forever Heroes* preserves 21 stories for future generations to learn about what WWII was like. It is a gift from Dr. Winfield to all Nebraskans."

> — Bill and Evonne Williams
> Patriotic Productions

"After reading *Forever Heroes* and wiping away tears, I was reminded why I am indeed proud to be an American. History is not discovered in tidy books of dates and events, but rather in the telling of actual stories that preserve memories. This is reality and these World War II stories that illustrate great character and the American spirit need to be read."
— Jeff Kappeler, Executive Director
Dodge County Historical Society

"Joyce Winfield brought to life some of the greatest stories of the Greatest Generation. Many of these stories would never have been told had it not been for her taking such an interest in the experiences of these men and women. As teenagers and young adults in the early 1940s, these World War II veterans were proud to serve their country. *Forever Heroes* reinforces why, in turn, everyone should be proud of them."
— Stan Vyhlidal, Commander
American Legion Post 20, Fremont, Neb.

"As young men and women, they went to war. In the decades after, some bore wounds and all carried memories. Now in their 90s, in stories to be cherished, they have shared with Joyce Winfield their experiences — their fears, sacrifices, adventures, and triumphs — in an increasingly distant conflict. These acts of remembering are perhaps their final service."
— Fred Nielsen, Department of History
University of Nebraska at Omaha

FOREVER HEROES

<><><><><><><><><><><><><><><><>

A Collection
of
World War II Stories
from
Nebraska Veterans

Joyce H. Winfield, Ph.D.

Prairieland Press

Prairieland Press™

P. O. Box 2404
Fremont, NE 68026-2404
www.PrairielandPress.com

Ordering Information:
Quantity sales. Special discounts are available on quantity purchases by corporations, associations, and others. For details, contact the publisher at the address above.

Printed in the United States of America

Publisher's Cataloging-in-Publication data
Names: Winfield, Joyce H.
Title: Forever heroes : a collection of World War II stories from Nebraska veterans / Joyce H. Winfield, Ph. D.
Description: First Trade Original Edition | Fremont, NB: Prairieland Press, 2017.
Identifiers: ISBN 978-1-944132-02-6 (pbk.) | 978-1-944132-03-3 (ebook) | LCCN 2016949807
Subjects: LCSH World War, 1939-1945--Nebraska--Biography. | United States--Armed Forces--Biography. | Veterans—Nebraska—Biography. | Veterans--Nebraska--Personal narratives. | BISAC BIOGRAPHY & AUTOBIOGRAPHY / Military | HISTORY / United States / State & Local / Midwest (IA, IL, IN, KS, MI, MN, MO, ND, NE, OH, SD, WI) | HISTORY / United States / 20th Century
Classification: LCC U52 .W56 2017 | DDC 978.2--dc23

I will Forever Miss
my three Uncles
whose World War II stories
I never got to tell:

Lee Gissler, Army Air Forces
Rol Gissler, Army
Wilmer Johnson, Army Air Forces

And Bert Gissler, my Dad,
whose love of history
became my love of history

CONTENTS

INTRODUCTION

Seventy-five years ago, on Dec. 7, 1941, Japanese fighter planes attacked Pearl Harbor, drawing the United States into World War II. An estimated 16 million Americans served during the war, including 21 whose stories are told in *Forever Heroes: A Collection of World War II Stories from Nebraska Veterans*. In the 1940s, the ages of my veterans ranged from 17 to 24. Today, their ages range from 89 to 96. According to the National WWII Museum website: "Approximately every three minutes a memory of World War II — its sights and sounds, its terrors and triumphs — disappears. Yielding to the inalterable process of aging, the men and women who fought and won the great conflict are now mostly in their 90s. They are dying quickly — at the rate of approximately 430 a day, according to U.S. Veterans Administration figures."

It has been my privilege to be the storyteller for 21 amazing stories. I never planned to write a book that relates the experiences of World War II veterans. Maybe I would write the story of one veteran who served in three wars.

It all started with coffee and a cap. I was with two writer friends, Cheryl and Nancy, at a local Fremont, Nebraska, fast-food restaurant on Nov. 16, 2015. We meet about every two weeks to encourage and support each other in our writing endeavors. I had just shared that I was in a writing slump. It had taken me almost six months to finish my last short article.

I was currently unmotivated and nothing interested me as a potential writing project.

It was time for a coffee refill, so I stood and faced the coffee dispensers. That's when I first saw the cap. An older man was sitting directly to my left. He was wearing a black cap with "WWII - Korea - Vietnam Veteran" stitched in gold. I had seen many veterans wearing Korea and Vietnam caps, and I had even seen some for WWII. But, I had never seen all three on one cap. As I walked toward the table, the man looked up.

"I love your cap. One doesn't see many like yours." I thanked him for his service and told him my husband, Doug, is a Vietnam veteran. His response was to thank me for thanking him. A woman also sitting at the table interjected with a British accent, "He was in the service for 26 years." Before I could react, the man replied, "Guess I was doing such a good job, they kept sending me back."

Veteran's Day had been five days earlier, so I mentioned that Doug and I had attended two programs in town. The woman said they live in Uehling (21 miles north of Fremont) and had not participated in any Veteran's Day activities. After her comment, I wished them a good day and left to get my refill. When I was finishing that second cup of coffee, I saw the man stand and reach for a nearby walker. I got one last glimpse of his cap.

I could not get that cap out of my mind. I kept thinking, "That man has a story to tell." How difficult could it be to find a three-war veteran in Uehling, Nebraska, population 223? On

Nov. 20, Doug and I drove to Uehling. I found three men having coffee around 9 a.m. and, as soon as I described the cap, they all knew I was looking for Alvin Cooper. He was no longer the man with the three-war cap; he had a name. One of the men called the Coopers and Doug and I were told to come right over. The man who made the phone call had us follow his truck to the home of Alvin and Mona Cooper. That entire scenario could only happen in a small town.

Before I left the Coopers that first time, I made arrangements to return on Dec. 10 and interview 90-year-old Alvin about his 26-year military career. I love history and listening to Alvin talk about his experiences was educational and enlightening.

On Dec. 18, I met again with Cheryl and Nancy; I told them how excited I was to be writing Alvin Cooper's story. A subsequent comment and a question from Nancy changed everything. "My dad is a World War II veteran. Would you write his story?" Cheryl added that I should interview other World War II veterans and write a book.

So began the project that pulled me from a writing slump. I had no predetermined method for finding veterans, and there was nothing significant about selecting 21. Friends, neighbors, and members of my church and organizations that I have joined shared names of veterans they knew. Those veterans suggested other veterans. A well laid-out plan maybe would have resulted in more than two women, but that's OK. My not well laid-out plan resulted in more Army veterans, but that's also OK. My 21 includes veterans who were in the

Army, Army Nurse Corps, Marine Corps, Navy, a WAVE and a Merchant Marine. Six were drafted and 15 enlisted. More than one veteran said to me, "I didn't do much." Well, in my book, everybody's job was equally important.

Every evening, I write in a small book titled *The Happiness Project: One-Sentence Journal*. It was a gift from JoAnne, my sister, and each date has an entry from the author. On Jan. 5, which is my Dad's birthday, it says, "When life is taking its ordinary course, it's hard to remember what matters. If you want a happiness project, you have to make the time." So, from the beginning, I made time for *Forever Heroes* — my Happiness Project. This doesn't mean that I never shed tears, but at the end of most days I was able to smile.

My first interview focusing only on World War II involvement was Jan. 11. With that interview, I turned *Forever Heroes* over to the Lord and He led me throughout the entire process. After sharing my frustration with Nancy and Cheryl about being in a writing slump and then seeing Alvin Cooper with his cap, He made it obvious to me. "Nothing to write about? I'll give you something to write about." And He sure did.

I feel it's necessary to mention memories. My oldest veteran entered the service in November 1941 and the rest followed from 1942-45. They were asked to remember occurrences that happened seven decades ago. Some of my questions were followed by silence and then, "I don't remember." If something couldn't be included in their stories because of that response, it didn't matter. Also, my veterans shared either a formal or informal service picture that was used on the cover and the first page of their stories. Are they in less-than-perfect condition? Yes, but it didn't matter. Just like their memories, their photos are more than 70 years old.

I've spent so much time with my veterans, they feel like family. And, yes, I always refer to them as "my veterans." Initial interviews, follow-up questions and photos were all scheduled. Other times I stopped by because I had one more question or I needed clarification regarding previous responses. Sometimes, it wasn't as simple as making a phone call. Some of my veterans have hearing loss and, for many, it's a consequence of the war. They simply did not like talking on the phone. So, needing one question answered became a morning or afternoon of chatting and coffee. I've shared birthdays with them and even attended a 70th wedding anniversary reception. Seventy years!

Having these 21 veterans become a significant part of my life has been a joy — thanks to the Lord. They all are humble about their service and they all were proud to serve. They had few regrets. But I have regrets. I've dedicated *Forever Heroes* to my Uncle Lee, Uncle Rol and Uncle Wilmer. They served during World War II but, before they died, I didn't talk to any of them about their service. Others should learn from my regrets. I'm urging anyone who knows relatives, friends or neighbors who are veterans — and not just World War II — or who are active duty military to take time and thank them. Also, ask if they would share their stories. We must never forget what they have sacrificed for our freedom.

Each day when I prepared to work at the dining room

table, I looked at a picture I had placed on a small chest. "Heroes don't wear capes, they wear dog tags." Writing this book has definitely reinforced that these veterans are *Forever Heroes*. And now, as a result of *Forever Heroes*, I have Forever Friends.

◇◇◇◇◇◇◇◇◇◇◇◇◇◇◇◇◇◇◇◇◇◇◇◇

During the first visit with each veteran, I left a biographical form to be completed. Included was a space for branch of service. Responses were used when writing the veteran's story and also for the informational box below the service picture on the first page of each story.

Regarding Army Air Corps and Army Air Forces, the following information will serve as clarification. Retired Colonel C.C. Elebash, U.S. Air Force, wrote: "U.S. Army personnel have traditionally been assigned to branches: Infantry, Artillery, Air Corps, Quartermaster Corps, Corps of Engineers, etc. The Army Air Forces (AAF) came into being on June 20, 1941, six months before Pearl Harbor. World War II Air Corps personnel had a strong sentimental attachment to their branch. Many WWII servicemen still proudly identify themselves as veterans of the Air Corps. However — although the Air Corps was their branch — they actually served and fought in the Army Air Forces. In honoring Army aviation in WWII, the most appropriate and inclusive identification is Army Air Forces."

Whichever a veteran wrote — Army Air Corps or Army Air Forces — that is what I included with his story.

William Barnhart
Navy

◇◇◇◇◇◇◇◇◇◇◇◇◇◇◇◇◇◇◇◇◇◇◇◇

Birth Date:
Jan. 28, 1925

Hometown:
Monsanto, Ill.

Age When Enlisted:
17

Service Dates:
November 1942 –
January 1946

Highest Rank:
Chief Sonarman

Before Bill Barnhart, 91, became a Navy sonarman, he was a barber, a quarter-of-beef lifter, a deck-sweeper and a line splicer. In addition to his memories of these jobs, he acquired a permanent and physical reminder of the Navy.

At age 17 in November 1942, Barnhart enlisted in the Navy because of his hero, a cousin who had joined the Navy. Leaving Monsanto, Illinois, where he lived with his father and sister, he arrived at boot camp at Naval Station Great Lakes in North Chicago. There he became a barber.

Before their first haircuts, the men tried to get a good night's sleep after the train arrived at Great Lakes around 10 p.m. "We were put in an auditorium with a bunch of stanchion supports that held hammocks." Noting there were 120 hammocks in the auditorium, Barnhart asked, "Ever tried to sleep in a hammock if it's too tight? It will just flip you out. These guys would be flipped out and everybody would start laughing." Even though he never was flipped out of his hammock, Barnhart got very little sleep that night. Helping to assure he would stay in the hammock, he positioned himself on his stomach and grabbed hold of the hammock next to him.

When the 120 men were ready for haircuts, the men stood in line alphabetically. Barnhart was one of the first six at the head of the line. Those six were told to go stand behind a barber's chair. "We were told to buzz it off. We all looked the same." After all the men received haircuts, Barnhart's stint as a barber ended.

After nine weeks at boot camp, half of his original unit of 120 men were sent to Philadelphia. His second job also lasted only a day. "We were outfitting an aircraft carrier. I had a heck of a time carrying a quarter of beef up ladders. Men were dropping them and grease was on the ladders. It was terrible."

Barnhart soon was assigned to a ship that was commissioned on April 7, 1943. The USS PC-1196 (patrol craft) was docked in Brooklyn, New York. He described the ship as 164-feet long, like a mini-destroyer, real narrow and "rougher than a cob."

Outside New York Harbor was the next stop for Barnhart's ship where barges hauled shells and other ammunition to be loaded on the mini-destroyer. After leaving the harbor, stops included: Miami, Florida; Havana, Cuba; and finally the United States Naval Station at Guantanamo (Gitmo) Bay, Cuba. While on ship, the men participated in a variety of drills. "By the time you go to sleep, then they start those drills. They go through every one of them. You learn." He emphasized, "They're teaching you when something happens, you know what to do." The stops at Havana and Gitmo were for rest and relaxation (R&R). Time was needed off ship. "They trained us pretty hard. We had to have a little rest because our home was on that ship." Part of the relaxation was a rum & Coke that cost 15 cents.

Barnhart started on the PC-1196 as a seaman deuce, which is "the very lowest seaman there is." As soon as he got on the ship, he began striking. That meant he was looking for a permanent job. In the meantime, his first job on the ship was on the port side. "I'd sweep the deck from the bow to the stern and then I'd walk back up there and start over again and sweep."

What happened next, Barnhart said, was the best thing that happened during his time in the Navy. When he was sweeping, he stopped midships (middle section of the ship) where a chief boatswain's mate was outfitting a life raft. A boatswain's mate trains, directs and supervises personnel in ship's maintenance duties. "He looked up at me and said, 'Barnhart, how would you like to learn how to splice line?' I said great and he hollered at somebody else and gave him my broom."

Splicing increased the strength of a rope that was woven through loops around life rafts. Anyone in the water could then hold on to the loops. Barnhart continued splicing for about two days, and he said that splicing line was a job that gave him purpose to get up every morning. "Before that I could sleep after reveille [loud speaker announcement]. I couldn't wake up. But after I started splicing line, I was up before reveille every morning."

Next came the opportunity leading to the position Barnhart held until the end of his service in 1946. "I was standing watch, out on the bow. A sonarman was also there. I was always looking for something better than standing out and freezing my butt off." Over the next six to eight months and with on-the-job training, Barnhart became a sonarman. Sonar (SOund Navigation And Ranging) detected and located German submarines by sending sound waves underwater. Sound pulses called pings could travel 4,000 yards, hit an object and send a returning sound echo. The PC-1196 had one sonar machine, located on the ship's bridge that is the room from which the ship is navigated. One man operated the sonar machine; however, there were three sonarmen on ship who covered three shifts.

On the sonar machine screen, Barnhart tracked the returning echoes. Length of time that elapsed between sending the signal and hearing the returning echo determined a submarine's location. "When an area on the sonar machine got really wide that meant you were a little closer to the submarine. That's when we would drop our depth charges." The depth charges were barrel-shaped drums filled with 550 pounds of TNT positioned on a rack on each side of the ship's fantail. While the ship kept moving, someone yelled "Fire 1." Two drums simultaneously were rolled off each side. "Fire 2" repeated the action. This continued until maybe 24 depth charges were released.

At the same time the drums were falling, Barnhart said K-guns (depth charge projectors) threw depth charges to the side. "When they fire that, it goes up in the air and over about 75 feet and drops off. When you do that with two of them, it takes care of that area on both sides." Together, the drums and K-guns dropped a pattern of 9 or 10 charges.

The ship's skipper was kept abreast of sonar readings and he decided what action would be taken. Barnhart doesn't know if any depth charges destroyed submarines. "I spent almost three years on that ship and the skipper never said anything. He was mum." For two of those three years, the PC-1196 traveled to many of the small islands in the eastern Caribbean. "Going to these different islands, we were looking for German bases but never found any."

After the aforementioned R&R stops, the PC-1196 entered its first convoy that included Merchant Marine supply ships traveling to Trinidad. The PC-1196 and another patrol craft were responsible for protecting the supply ships. One patrol craft was positioned on each side of the convoy. "We were way out from them [supply ships]. Our job was to make sure we would get the subs before they got into the convoy." Two other sonarmen and Barnhart each alternated duty shifts, four hours on and four hours off.

It took the convoy about 10 days to reach Trinidad with an average speed of 8 knots (9.2 miles per hour). Only the patrol crafts moved in a zigzag pattern, and Barnhart continually turned the sonar machine wheel, scanning specific areas of the ocean for submarines.

Because the convoy was constantly moving from one island to another, mail delivery was erratic. Barnhart received few letters from home and he sent few letters. "We weren't allowed to tell where we were and an officer would go through the letters and say, 'Cut out this, cut out that.'" Referred to as V-mail, short for Victory Mail, the method allowed for faster, less expensive correspondence. After the letters were censored, they were transferred to microfilm. After the letters reached their destinations, the negatives were increased to full size and printed. According to the National WWII Museum website, "Using this small microfilm saved the postal system thousands of tons of shipping space, fitting the equivalent of 37 mail bags worth of letters into just one."

Mail wasn't the only thing in short supply on the ship. Any kind of food that would quickly spoil was not on board. "We had eggs that were frozen in 1938. Said that on the case of eggs. Figure that out. Guess they can keep frozen eggs a long time." Barnhart said food on the ship was good, including lots of navy beans. His first breakfast at boot camp featured navy beans and grapefruit. "I like beans but the grapefruit didn't go well with beans."

Just before the PC-1196 was ready to leave Puerto Rico

in August 1945 for the Pacific, a crank shaft broke. Barnhart and Mac, another sonarman, volunteered for permanent shore patrol while the ship was being repaired in San Juan. That is when he heard that Japan had surrendered on Sept. 2, 1945. The news resulted in celebration on the ship. Barnhart explained any man on shore patrol "could walk into a bar and say, 'I want that bottle,' and they would give him the bottle — no money." When the war ended, it was before payday. So, Barnhart and Mac went to bars in San Juan and got a bottle of whiskey at each place. When they arrived back on the ship, they put all the bottles in one place. "We supplied the drinks."

From September 1945 until he was discharged in January 1946, Barnhart was on permanent shore patrol in San Juan. When he enlisted in November 1942, his commitment with the Navy was for two years and duration of the war. With so many servicemen and women eligible for discharge when the war ended, it took the extra few months for Barnhart to get discharged.

Getting those free bottles of whiskey in San Juan is a memory of Barnhart's naval days in Puerto Rico at the end of the war. However, he also has that permanent and physical reminder of Puerto Rico from earlier in the war. "I was 19. I was with two other guys and we'd been drinking." On his right arm, stretching just below his elbow to his wrist is a tattoo of a hula girl. "I got a big one and I don't know why. They brought it up." Always blame the other guys.

◇◇◇◇◇◇◇◇◇◇◇◇◇◇◇◇◇◇◇

After the war, Barnhart remained in the Naval Reserves. He worked at a Hormel Foods meat-packing plant in Fremont, Nebraska, for 37½ years. He retired in 1985. During the Korean War, Barnhart went back to active duty as a sonarman. He served 37 years in the Navy, including both active and reservist duty. Barnhart reached the military mandatory retirement age of 60 in 1985.

Bill and Ilene Barnhart live in Fremont, Nebraska, and have been married 70 years. Their wedding date is June 15, 1946. The Barnharts have 2 sons, Bill and Don; 5 grandchildren; and 8 great-grandchildren.

Raymond "Red" Carstensen

Army

◇◇◇◇◇◇◇◇◇◇◇◇◇◇◇◇◇◇◇◇

Birth Date:
May 13, 1921

Hometown:
Bennington, Neb.

Age When Enlisted:
24

Service Dates:
September 1944 –
October 1945

Highest Rank:
Private

Ray "Red" Carstensen, 95, remembered two great buddies when he was stationed in the Army at Fort Robinson in northwest Nebraska. Their names were King and Sandy. They both had four legs.

Carstensen knew lots of four-legged animals. His father raised hogs on a farm near Uehling, Nebraska. When Carstensen was just shy of his 16th birthday, his father became ill with pneumonia. As the only son with seven sisters, he left high school to help on the family farm. For the next eight years, he tended the livestock, not just hogs, but also horses, cows and the family dogs. Shep was an English shepherd and Brownie was a Heinz 57.

At age 23 in September 1944, he selected the Army

because "it was the first thing that came to my mind. What the heck?" Referring to the deferments he had received to remain home and help on the farm, Carstensen said, "I had the only draft card in Dodge County that had no expiration date on it."

Loaded with troops, Carstensen's train headed south and made a 4-day stop at Fort Leavenworth, Kansas. Carstensen was inducted into the Army on Sept. 21. His next destination was Camp Robinson in North Little Rock, Arkansas, for basic training.

Target practice, of course, was a key component of basic training. For Carstensen, that was a problem. "I'm left-handed and had to shoot left-handed and the Army didn't like that." He explained the M1 rifles and machine guns used for practice had all the casings fly out to the right. Being left-handed, with a dominant left eye, meant the casings went across his face left to right. For right-handed shooters with dominant right eyes, the casings did not fly across their faces. "I told them all if they wanted me to shoot right-handed, they better get behind me because I didn't know where the casing would go."

Also during basic training, there was an incident with a hand grenade. "We threw dummies all the time and then went to live. There was a trench with planks that you walked on and threw the grenades over." He then explained that one man pulled a grenade pin and just froze. "There's a live grenade in his hand. A sergeant was on his right and I'm on his left. The sergeant got there first and gave it [the hand grenade] a push and it exploded about 4 feet from my head." Hearing loss in his right ear is a result of the explosion.

Running in basic training created another challenge. "Me and my big mouth." On the first day, the 200 men in Company B were told they were going to run a 6-minute mile. "There were all these young 18-year-olds. You never heard so much moaning and groaning." Carstensen spoke up and admitted he had never run a 4-minute mile but said he could probably do it in a little more than 5 minutes. "You think so?" That was a lieutenant who responded.

Next thing Carstensen knew, he and a sergeant were at a starting point. "So we start down a hill and then we go up a little slope and then we go down a little bit more and then we turn and we go up just a bit and go down some more and then up and down. Then we make a turn and the last quarter of a mile is one of the Arkansas hills straight up." The sergeant set the pace and Carstensen stayed with him. Back at the starting point, Carstensen was pleased to report to the other men the time was 5 minutes. "So, 6 minutes should be fairly easy." So, everyone — including Carstensen — ran the same mile again. "Still didn't teach me to keep my mouth shut."

Not keeping his mouth shut possibly affected his next destination after eight weeks of basic training. It was the last night at Camp Robinson and Company B was ready for its last 26-mile march. "I'm standing there, leaning against my Browning Automatic Rifle. It was dark already, a jeep pulls up and someone calls out my name." Back at head-quarters, Carstensen answered one question after another. Calling the process an interrogation, he joined nine other men for an assignment at Fort Robinson, Nebraska. He would be a training instructor with the K-9 Corps. Why Fort Robinson? Fort Robinson was a site where the U.S. Army Remount Service was operating. Since the Civil War the Service had provided horses (and later mules) to Army units. During World War II, dogs received training for scout, sentry, messenger, sled and pack duties.

The 10 men from Camp Robinson in Arkansas headed for Fort Robinson in Nebraska aboard a train that stopped in Oklahoma and Kansas. The MPs (military police) in Kansas City greeted the men at the railroad depot. "There's the guys going to the dogs." Since they had to wait for their next train, the men left the depot. "I never get lost, but I couldn't remember where we were." When a cab driver stopped, Carstensen said the men were only a couple of blocks from the depot. "Now there's 10 guys getting into that cab. Two were on the front fender, the back doors weren't closed and you should have heard the MPs laugh when we got back."

Arriving at Fort Robinson in January 1945, there was snow on the ground. Dogs and their handlers after eight weeks of training would be sent to a Pacific island. "I don't know what island, but it didn't make sense that we were training here in the snow." On the islands, dogs and handlers could be the first on the beach to lead a company or platoon into the jungle. "The dogs could pick up a scent of anybody within a half mile. Those dogs did not bark, did not make a sound. They were trained to attack."

Carstensen spent 18 months at Fort Robinson, but his training responsibilities focused not on the scout dogs but the men who handled the dogs. Five training centers were established across the U.S. in 1942-43. In September 1942, Fort Robinson became the largest remount station serving the Midwest. Nearly 5,000 dogs, half the number used during the war, were trained at Fort Robinson. Many were donated from pet owners across the country. After the bombing at Pearl Harbor, a nationwide organization spearheaded the canine and handler training effort in support of the war. Puppies and older dogs were not accepted. "The dogs would have to be in their prime."

During its three years of operation, Dogs for Defense obtained approximately 18,000 dogs through donations. Included were a poodle from Greer Garson (actress) and a German shepherd from Mary Pickford (actress). After the war, or if a dog was not successful in the Dogs for Defense program, the organization attempted to return the dog to its owner. "They would try their darnedest to get the dogs back home."

At Fort Robinson, Carstensen worked with King, whose owner was Rudy Vallee (singer, actor and bandleader). King, a male Doberman, was "black as black can be." Age unknown, King was 29 inches tall at the shoulders and weighed 84 pounds. Carstensen described King as faithful. "He was just a plain good dog. What he would do one day, he would do the next day." Carstensen didn't know if King was returned to Vallee after the war.

While training the handlers, each of the seven instructors consistently worked with the same two dogs. In addition to King, Carstensen had Sandy, a male German shepherd/chow cross who was the color of sand. A chow body and German shepherd temperament is how Carstensen described Sandy. "He was about half the size of King and probably weighed at least 50 pounds. He was solid as a rock but he could jump." Carstensen knew nothing about Sandy's background, but he added that the dog would attack anything and not back away.

Other men at Fort Robinson were responsible for training the dogs. Learning to obey verbal commands and gestures was emphasized. The dogs also had to become accustomed to wearing muzzles and gas masks, riding in vehicles and working under gunfire. The handlers learned about grooming, feeding, kenneling and the capabilities and limitations of their dogs. Teamwork was key, as well as patience and repetition. "Nothing happens in one day." Noting that the dog really was in charge, Carstensen said, "If you couldn't read your dog or know what your dog was telling you, you were in deep trouble."

Standard equipment during training included a leash and a harness. Working daily with the dogs resulted in Carstensen and another handler designing a prototype for an adjustable harness. It was approved and became the standard issue for the training harness. Training sessions for the dogs and handlers lasted eight weeks. Estimating he worked with 20-25 handlers and 40-50 dogs, Carstensen added, "If dogs got out of line, most of the time it was the handler's fault."

Using either King or Sandy during training sessions, Carstensen selected locations for someone to stand as decoys. Picking up the decoy's scent, King or Sandy reacted and each handler made written notes of the dog's actions. "When the dog would pick up the scent, he would stop, turn and his nose would be pointing right at you. If you go further over, there probably would be another place with a scent and he would turn back. Where those lines crossed, 99 percent of the time, that's where the decoys were."

To simulate combat situations, men and dogs participated in exercises that officers observed and then provided feedback. On March 14, 1945, Carstensen and Sandy teamed with a patrol leader and two riflemen. With clear weather and favorable wind conditions, man and dog were rated on three scenarios. Sergeant Tyler's written remarks were, "Handler and Dog both did a very good job of patrolling." That meant Sandy successfully picked up the scents.

In addition to review from the base officers at Fort Robinson, Carstensen and his dogs also gave many demonstrations for dignitaries. Curtis LeMay was one of those men. When the U.S. entered the war after the attack on Pearl Harbor, LeMay led the 8th Air Force. In early 1942, he was in command of the 305th Bomb Group and its bombing missions over Europe. "I got King and saw this jeep and knew it was LeMay because he had a cigar in his mouth."

After King successfully picked up the scent of one decoy, Carstensen felt he should continue because LeMay's visit could be an example of when a double decoy had been set up. "If I didn't go, then I'd really catch it. So, I went on and sure enough they had a double." Carstensen said LeMay was very impressed and didn't realize King would be able to pick up a scent half a mile away.

As publicity for the K-9 Corps, Carstensen and Sandy were filmed for a promotional piece to be shown in movie theaters. "I had to stop and get new fatigues and ended up wading through water and Sandy is swimming right beside me. Then I had to get down and crawl along the sand. A demolition man had set in little quarter pounds of nitro-starch. [Nitrostarch is a secondary explosive made by mix-ing sulfuric acid and nitric acid.] He had it lined up with little spots on the sand. That's where I had to line up and crawl. Sandy was crawling, too. They were setting those off so it looked like shell fire. It never bothered Sandy." Carstensen never saw the final film. But his sister, brother-in-law and young nephew were watching a movie in Gretna, Nebraska, when Henry said, "That's Uncle Ray!"

A German prisoner of war camp was located about 2 miles from Fort Robinson. One evening Carstensen was called out of a movie theater after a prisoner had escaped. Because Sandy worked better at night than King, Carstensen took Sandy and a .45 pistol. "That was the only time I carried live ammunition." Sandy never did pick up the scent of the prisoner, who was later found in York, Nebraska, 375 miles southeast of Fort Robinson.

Two months after the Japanese surrendered (Aug. 15, 1945), Carstensen was called into the captain's office on Thursday, Oct. 18. "He reached into his file and takes the top paper and hands it to me. It was a dependency discharge." Every month Carstensen sent $35 of his $64 pay home to his parents, which they used to make payments on the farm. "The captain knew how much I sent home. I didn't have hardly anything left each month."

His parents had to gather affidavits stating Carstensen was needed at home. "I got the papers on the 20th [October], left on the 22nd and stopped at Fort Carson in Colorado Springs, Colorado, on the 23rd, where I got my discharge." From the time he learned he was being discharged, "Everything happened so fast it was pitiful." Noting men could wait months to get paperwork for discharge, he couldn't believe how quickly he was on an Army bus from the base to Crawford, Nebraska, and then a train to Colorado.

"I never regret one minute of the time I spent in the service. I hope that I did something good." Actually there was a regret, a lasting regret that involved his four-legged buddies. "I never got to say goodbye to King and Sandy."

After the war, Carstensen raised and trained hunting dogs; worked as a carpenter with his future father-in-law; farmed for 19 years outside Hooper, Nebraska; and worked in the Midland Lutheran College (Fremont, Nebraska) Maintenance Department for 19 years. He retired in 1987.

Ray "Red" Carstensen lives in Fremont, Nebraska, and was married to Elaine for 56 years. Their wedding date is Sept. 15, 1950. They have 1 son, Dean, and 1 daughter, Laraine; and 3 grandchildren.

Alvin Cooper
Army Air Corps

◇◇◇◇◇◇◇◇◇◇◇◇◇◇◇◇◇◇◇◇◇◇◇◇

Birth Date:
Feb. 4, 1925

Hometown:
North Platte, Neb.

Age When Enlisted:
18

Service Dates:
June 1943 –
December 1945

Highest Rank:
Master Sergeant E8

Stationed for 13 months on an island about 2 miles long and 2 miles wide, Alvin Cooper, 91, lived where there are as many as 250 rainy days a year and as few as eight clear days. That was the weather pattern on Shemya Island.

Shemya Island is located at the end of the Aleutian Island chain in the Pacific Ocean. Cooper served the majority of his time as a radio operator on a B-24 Liberator with the 404th Bombardment Squadron, 11th Army Air Force. He remembered about 12 planes having the Aleutian Islands as home base. "We used to fly to the Kuril Islands, which is near Japan, for bombing missions." Military installations were the targets.

The B-24 encountered Japanese fighters "primarily

to make sure we didn't get on the mainland of Japan." Since the Kuril Islands are just 200 miles from Russia, Cooper added, "Of course, the Russian fighters also met us 20 miles off their coast to escort us and make sure we didn't get too close to Russia." He doesn't remember experiencing much opposition from the Japanese. "But, they were present and flying just out of .50-caliber range [2,000 yards]."

Depending on the B-24 model, 7-10 men were assembled to form a crew. Positions included: pilot, co-pilot, nose gunner, bombardier, navigator, dorsal turret gunner (also doubled as the flight engineer), tail gunner, waist gunners (both left and right positions) and radio operator.

The navigator also was from Nebraska. "Frank B. Sloan from Geneva always brought us back to base, although we would probably be very low on fuel."

As radio operator, Cooper's position in the B-24 was right behind the pilot. Because of the cold temperature, the crew always wore heated suits. When the plane rose above the clouds, "that's when we could see the sun."

He stated, "I had to keep in contact with home base and send position reports." The navigator relayed locations of the B-24 to the radio operator. Keeping his headset on for hours, Cooper listened for friendly communications, reported situational updates to the navigator and updated headquarters on mission results. He logged all relevant action.

When radio contact with home base was lost, sometimes it was possible to communicate with a nearby fishing boat. If that boat was on the same frequency as the B-24, "maybe that fishing boat could contact base." Stormy weather and equipment failure were main reasons for radio communications failure.

Radio operators on the B-24 could also assume one of the waist gunner positions if needed. This happened when enemy aircraft had been detected. Standing in an open bay window, Cooper manned a belt-fed .50-caliber machine gun. The B-24 could also carry eight bombs (four on each side), depending on their size and fuel requirement.

At times, he released thin strips of shredded metal, called chaff, to confuse enemy radar. These strips were fired from a gun and the metal deflected off enemy radar since the chaff could be detected on a radar scope. "It didn't take them long to determine it wasn't another aircraft."

Referring to enemy attacks, Cooper defined flak, or ack-ack, as anti-aircraft gunfire. "Our bomb runs were usually made at an altitude of about 17,000 feet. This altitude seemed to be the level at which Japanese ack-ack became a little less accurate."

He explained the B-24 always carried flak jackets for the bomber crews to wear. "But I remember when we made a bombing run, we used to take the flak jackets off and lay them on the floor. That's because most of the flak was underneath and it would come up through the floor."

Roundtrip for a mission from Shemya Island to the Kuril Islands took 10-12 hours. Since it got pretty noisy in the B-24, some crew members read magazines or talked to each other through earphones. "The long flights to the target were a bit monotonous to some crew members but not to me." Cooper described radio communication aboard military aircraft being accomplished on CW (continuous waveform) high frequency by use of a telegraph key. CW communication means turning on and off a radio signal to make long and short pulses. All transmissions had to be coded and decoded. "Sending messages by key from an aircraft in turbulent weather was not an easy task."

Although Cooper felt his B-24 was never in danger of being shot down, he admitted having close calls when returning to home base. "Quite often we were running pretty low on fuel. So, if you call getting low on fuel a 'close call,' I suppose that would be."

The crew always had to be concerned about weather on the Aleutian Islands. Cooper noted, "It's foggy all the time." He emphasized, "When a plane was downed on a mission, it was more often because of the weather and not by enemy fire."

Another problem was the short runway. So in addition to fighting fog, the pilot frequently had to make several different runway approaches. "There probably was some praying."

Some pilots knew they wouldn't be able to make a safe landing. "We lost a couple of B-24s in the Aleutian Islands because they ran out of fuel and had no alternative but to ditch the aircraft off the coast and let the air-sea rescue bring them in. I always felt one day we would run out of fuel coming back and it would be the same thing for us."

Once back on base, a debriefing completed every mission. "Each crew member was encouraged to talk about how his part went in the mission and what he had seen. Part of the ritual was receiving a certificate from the squadron medical officer stating that you had flown a mission and were not required to fly again that day."

The medical slip could be exchanged for 3 ounces of whiskey that was dispensed at a nearby table. Or the slip could be given to someone, "if you were not a drinking man." Cooper admitted most men probably kept their slips and redeemed them for the whiskey because "it would help calm our nerves."

When not flying missions, Cooper worked on radio equipment or attended training programs. "You had to be able to do a certain amount of work on the equipment. You were an operator most of the time, but if the equipment broke down, then you had to do some work as a mechanic."

Training had begun for Cooper when he enlisted in the Army Air Corps in June 1943 because he wanted to be a pilot. He had just graduated from North Platte (Nebraska) High School. As an 18 year old, he didn't want to wait and be drafted. So he selected the Aviation Cadet program but wasn't accepted. "The physical was very strict and I didn't have good depth perception." His next choice was radio operator. "I still got to fly, but not in the front seat."

Cooper admitted his first days in the service were rough. "I was just trying to figure out what was going to happen." Plenty happened when he spent time at stateside training bases in Wyoming, Mississippi, Texas, South Dakota, Arizona, Nebraska, Idaho, Montana and Alaska.

For 20 weeks, he attended Army Radio Technical Training School in Sioux Falls, South Dakota. But for Cooper, it wasn't just about radio equipment. For six weeks, he attended aerial gunnery school in Yuma, Arizona. That was necessary, he reiterated, because the radio operator on larger aircraft could step in as a waist gunner. That meant learning to operate the .50-caliber machine gun. Since each bomber was different, he was trained in the B-24 but also the B-17, B-26 and B-25.

Fifteen months after Cooper enlisted, he was back in Nebraska. In September 1944, he arrived at the Lincoln Army Air Field where his B-24 flight crew was assembled. "An interesting note is there were nearly 18,500 Liberators built between 1939 and 1945 and flown in combat by the Army Air Forces in all theaters."

The men then continued training as a combat air crew. Picking up its designated B-24, the crew completed transitional flight training in Idaho and Montana. Last stop before leaving the U.S. was Anchorage, Alaska, for instrument landing check-out.

In October 1944, the B-24 crew flew to Shemya. Weather conditions during training in the U.S. didn't prepare Cooper for those rainy, cloudy days on Shemya Island. Letters and packages from home helped ease homesickness. "I used to be a good letter writer and Mother used to write all the time." Packages from home were always welcomed. "Cookies. I think everyone in the service wanted their mom's cookies."

Meals on Shemya? "Of course, the food wasn't like Mom used to make, but it was good compared to C-rations." Especially enjoying breakfasts, Cooper said he liked the hot cakes and eggs. "I was never hungry."

Being based on an island meant there was no leave and not much entertainment. Still, he stressed there was little free time. "You work on the aircraft or go to training programs, so we didn't have much fun. There was lots of card playing."

Cooper noted there were few humorous or unusual events occurring on Shemya. "I never did drink or smoke." He laughed and quickly added, "Or run around with women because there weren't many women. Was that your next question?"

Twenty days before the end of the war, Cooper flew his last mission to the Kuril Islands on Aug. 13, 1945. When announcement of the end of the war arrived on Shemya Island over the radio, Cooper said, "I'm sure there were a lot of happy people, but I just don't remember."

However, he does remember when he was discharged on Dec. 26, 1945, after 30 months of service. He was going back to North Platte, where there were more than eight clear days a year.

After the war, Cooper had a military career focused on aviation that spanned 26 years, including 14 months in Korea and two tours in Vietnam. He retired from the military in 1969. As a civilian, Cooper was director of the Educational Technology Service Center at Troy State University (Troy, Alabama). Cooper also taught aircraft repair at Alabama Aviation and Technical College and was a tech inspector at Northrop Aircraft Facility at Fort Rucker. Cooper retired from his civilian career in 1988.

Alvin and Mona Cooper live in Uehling, Nebraska, and have been married for 60 years. Their wedding date is Oct. 3, 1956. Alvin is wearing his WWII - Korea - Vietnam Veteran cap that was the inspiration behind Forever Heroes.

Marvin Eden
Army Air Forces

◇◇◇◇◇◇◇◇◇◇◇◇◇◇◇◇◇◇◇◇

Birth Date:
May 4, 1922

Hometown:
Sterling, Neb.

Age When Drafted:
20

Service Dates:
September 1942 –
December 1945

Highest Rank:
Corporal

"Milne. M-i-l-n-e." "Moresby. M-o-r-e-s-b-y." "Biak. B-i-a-k." For each name, Marv Eden, 94, slowly and distinctly spelled each place where he was stationed between fall 1943 and winter 1945. The three locations are all located at the southern tip of New Guinea, part of the Pacific Theater.

His service began with the Army Air Forces on Sept. 17, 1942, after he received the official letter, which wasn't unexpected because he had registered for the draft on May 4, his birthday. Eden briefly summarized the letter's contents. "Greetings. Report to Fort Crook." He added, "I was the first bunch of 20-year-olds to be drafted." His basic training occurred at Kearns Army Air Base in Utah (13 miles outside Salt Lake City).

Prior to shipping out to New Guinea, Eden received advanced training in Oakland, California. "They had engines and electrical and hydraulics, all specialized. I was an electrician." Twenty men trained with Eden and he was one-tenth of a point short of being top of the class.

Milne Bay was Eden's first overseas destination when the USS *General John Pope* left Virginia. "We had no idea where we were going and we headed east. I thought, 'Oh my gosh, when we get to Europe I'm going to freeze my feet off.'"

Not knowing how long the troop replacement ship had been traveling east, at some point it turned south. Eden said he remembered thinking, "How in the world are we going to get to Europe?" Then the Panama Canal came into sight. The men were allowed on deck as the ship proceeded through the locks. A Nebraska farm boy from the southeastern part of the state, Eden said it was "fantastic" seeing the Panama Canal. "I'd never been out of Nebraska. Omaha was the farthest." Because the ship did not have an escort, it continued south in a zigzag pattern "so the Japanese wouldn't get a bead on us."

During 30 days on the ship, Eden was always hungry. The men were fed two meals a day — morning and evening. "There was a guy who carried a violin case aboard when we got on the ship. It was full of candy bars and he sold them for 50 cents." Determined he was not going to pay 50 cents for a nickel candy bar, his stomach was saying otherwise. "Pretty soon I was so hungry that I gave him 50 cents for a Snickers."

Close to 10 p.m. when the *General John Pope* docked in Milne Bay, the plan was to spend the night on the ship. However, Japanese bombers changed that plan. "The powers that be on that ship said, 'We have to get these men off of here.'" Eden estimated about 5,000 were aboard, 600-800 in his outfit. "Now, imagine getting off and it's pitch dark and you're going into the jungle. You carry one end of the pup tent and another guy carries the other end." As he visualized snakes, lizards, bugs and darkness, Eden said he wondered, "How are we going to do this?"

How to live in the jungle wasn't covered in basic training, but the jungles would be his home for about the next two years. Utilizing the beam from one flashlight for each tent, the men finished erecting their shelters when it started to rain. "I'm 6'4" and the tent isn't that long, so my feet were hanging out. I survived that."

The next day, the entire outfit left Milne Bay. About six or seven volunteers, including Eden, stayed behind to help load equipment. When that job was finished, there was only a B-24 left to transport the volunteers. "That's a big bomber. This young kid looked like he was in the 6th or 8th grade — and he was the pilot! The pilot had checked out the runway and said, 'If I can get to the end of the runway and get backed up some way, I think we can get off.'" Think? After takeoff, Eden said it looked like he could almost grab a handful of leaves. That's how close they were to the treetops.

In the islands around New Guinea, Eden had experience being close to the treetops as a member of the 60th Depot Repair Squadron. He climbed trees to string wire to buildings. Although his initial job had been wiring planes as an aircraft electrician, because of his height it was difficult for him to move around in the fuselage. So, he requested outside work and became a power lineman.

On New Guinea, he said: "The only source of electricity was big diesel generators. That was the power plant. We strung wire to the hangars where they were repairing planes. We put in transformer banks. We didn't get many good posts. Had to use trees and some of those trees were so hard I had to stomp my spikes to get up." Sometimes Eden climbed poles in the morning and didn't get down until noon.

He noted that sometimes it was difficult digging through coral on the islands. A 3-foot hole in the ground was needed for a 30-foot high pole; in addition to using shovels, Eden threw a half stick of dynamite into the hole.

Eden worked with six climbers/linemen. They wired officers' quarters and installed one light in each tent for the enlisted men. He estimated there were 20-30 tents that accommodated six men in each tent. Since he was on 24-hour duty, his crew had to be prepared at any time to repair lines destroyed by Japanese bombs. Because the Japanese usually targeted airstrips so the U.S. planes couldn't take off, the lines were not frequently damaged by enemy fire. He noted many planes that flew back to base were riddled with bullet holes. "The thing that was amazing is that you just took it in stride and did your job."

After leaving Milne Bay with the young pilot, Eden and his unit spent some time at Port Moresby. An airfield there was where men got experience flying in fighter planes and bombers. Aircraft repairs were made where possible. Some planes, however, couldn't be repaired and were ditched. "I can still see piles of airplanes junked just sitting there."

The island of Biak is southwest of New Guinea. "We were at Biak the longest time. Plane after plane took off from Biak — bombers and fighter escorts." The island is only 45 miles long and 23 miles wide, but it had three airbases. One night a Japanese bomber followed a hospital ship to the island and started firing. "If he had enough bombs, I wouldn't be here telling this. He had it aligned right straight across and we were right there 100 yards or less and he ran out of bombs just before where I was." That Japanese bomber was dropping daisy cutter bombs that sprayed shrapnel when they exploded. "I don't know how many we lost that night because there were tents and he just came across."

Three shots from an anti-aircraft gun were fired when Japanese bombers were spotted. "Maybe you wouldn't hear the first one, but you would hear the next two because it made a lot of noise." At the three-shot signal, the men grabbed their gas masks and headed for foxholes or behind rocks.

Another night, Eden saw a plane that was being tracked by lights on the ground. "The light was shining on the shiny belly and pretty soon I could see the bomb bay doors open. It was just black and then stuff coming out. I can see it yet." He added: "Our camp was only about 200 to 300 yards from the airstrip. They were aiming at the strip to disable it so our airplanes couldn't take off. Shrapnel was coming down everywhere." It was always the bombs and shrapnel that were the worst.

"Every time the Japanese would break through to our area, those in the outlying tents were given rifles. And I was always one who got a gun." Eden kept the loaded .30-caliber automatic rifle next to his cot. He credits his days growing up on a farm and loving to hunt as to why he got a rifle next to his cot on Biak. "A guy with me in the tent, Conway Frost, said to me 'Slim, I'll shine the light on them and you shoot.'"

While on Biak, Eden was able to see his older brother, Walter, who was serving with the 41st Infantry Division, field artillery. The brothers hadn't seen each other for at least two years and Eden got permission from his commanding officer to go find Walter. "I hitchhiked on all different kinds of planes." He finally found Walter in his mess hall and they had "quite a reunion for four or five days."

Eden emphasized that he developed a bond with men in his unit just like he had with Walter. "We were always together. It's a feeling that these guys are just part of your being. You get so close. You could trust them with your billfold and your life." In addition to Conway Frost, Eden mentioned Carlos Dey, William Epperson, Dean Geist, Cecil Johnson and Charles Perry as good friends.

When they weren't building, maintaining or repairing power lines or avoiding Japanese bombs and shrapnel, these buddies sometimes shared hot cocoa. "Coffee came in pretty big cans." The secret was to fill the can with a designated amount of water and then melt chocolate in it. "We'd have hot cocoa because we had a blow torch."

Forgetting the exact dates he arrived in Milne, Moresby and Biak, he knew the exact date he got back home. "It was the afternoon about 4 o'clock on Christmas Eve 1945. That was a good Christmas present." It was also a time when he finally cried. "I was just so happy. Just to get home when a lot of men didn't. And both Walter and I got home."

Eden talked a lot about his buddies and said it was important to enjoy some lighter moments. He called it frivolity. There was this wallaby that walked in a tent, got spooked and took off dragging behind it one of the men's mosquito nets. And there was this can of previously opened peaches that was left in a tent. A buddy took a big gulp and immediately spit it out, along with lots of black ants.

Sharing those stories now made Eden laugh — just like he laughed when the incidents happened more than 70 years ago. Frivolity is good. F-r-i-v-o-l-i-t-y.

After the war, Eden utilized the GI Bill and graduated from the University of Nebraska in Lincoln with a teaching degree. For two years, he taught Institutional on the Farm Training to veterans in Nebraska City. He sold agricultural chemicals for 10 years with Aller & Pease, Inc. in Beatrice, Nebraska. For 20 years, Eden was an agent for Federated Mutual Insurance Company. He retired in 1984.

Marv and Pat Eden live in Fremont, Nebraska, and have been married for 18 years. Their wedding date is June 20, 1998. Marv also was married to Wilma for 49½ years. They have 2 sons, Ronald and Verlyn; 5 grandchildren; and 4 great-grandchildren. Pat has 3 children, Steven, Beth, and Mark; and 5 grandchildren.

Benjamin Fischer
Army Air Corps

◇◇◇◇◇◇◇◇◇◇◇◇◇◇◇◇◇◇◇◇◇◇◇

Birth Date:
Jan. 26, 1920

Hometown:
Blair, Neb.

Age When Drafted:
21

Service Dates:
November 1941 –
December 1945

Highest Rank:
Sergeant

Ben Fischer, 96, was sleeping aboard the SS *Cape San Juan*, a U.S. freighter/troopship, when it was torpedoed by a Japanese submarine about 300 miles south of Fiji. It was Nov. 11, 1943, and about 5:30 in the morning when the torpedo hit. "I was below deck in the sleeping quarters. If that ship would have sunk right away, I wouldn't be talking to you now."

The torpedo hit a side of the *San Juan*, right about in the center. Sleeping quarters were in the front of the ship. "First thing I thought was that we got hit." Grabbing life jackets by their beds and bottles of water that could be attached to their belts, the men ran up to the deck. "The torpedo knocked the engine room out and the ship was

leaning to one side. Oil [from the ship's engines] was floating around and we were given orders to abandon ship."
After crawling down a rope ladder, Fischer began swimming toward a lifeboat and immediately became coated in
crude oil. Estimating about a third of those on the ship were
African Americans, Fischer said, "After being in the water
with crude oil all around, you couldn't tell a black guy from
a white guy."

Not knowing the number of available life rafts, Fischer
simply said, "I know they didn't have enough." Sources
recounting the sinking of the *San Juan* reported the ship
carried about six lifeboats, four large rafts and 36 smaller
rafts. Fischer swam toward a smaller life raft. He said maybe
four men were already on that raft; others kept swimming
toward it and crawling aboard. "It was a six-man life raft.
We had it packed so full that we couldn't get another person on." Final count was 33 men.

He chose to remain optimistic. "I always figured I was
going to get picked up. I never did give up. I realized there
would be a lot of people to be picked up. And it would take
time. And that's what it did. It took time." The life rafts
were framed with wood and covered with wood decking.
Barrels, which Fischer estimated to be about the size of
30-gallon drums, circled the perimeter of the raft.

When he first climbed into the raft, Fischer sat on a
barrel with both legs inside the raft. As more men climbed
aboard, everyone sitting on barrels switched positions. "We
straddled the barrel with one foot in the water and one foot

inside the raft. We could get more in that way. We were just as close as we could make it." More men were crouched on the floor of the raft. With 33 men on the raft, Fischer said: "The barrels didn't hold us up floating anymore. Our life jackets kept us floating."

No one in Fischer's life raft was injured. But he said one man kept saying: "I can't go any more. Oh, I can't." Fischer stated that man was ready to give up. "We talked him out of it." The life raft kept drifting until the *San Juan* was no longer in sight. And although the raft had paddles, the men didn't use them. "Where would we paddle to?"

There also were some K-rations in the raft. "We didn't know how old it was. Nobody ate them." The men had their water bottles, now covered with crude oil. Fischer chose not to drink from his. "I didn't get thirsty. I had other things on my mind."

The next day, Fischer saw a seaplane in the air that was picking up men who were floating in the ocean with just their lifejackets. He stressed it was right to rescue those men first. "I saw it up in the air, but we were too far away [for the pilot] to see us." He also added he never saw any sharks in the water and the crude oil probably kept them away.

Ships in the area headed toward where the *San Juan* was sinking. Men on a destroyer rescued Fischer and the other 32 men after they had been on the raft for 30 hours. Hungry and sleepy, he first wanted to take a shower. A sailor gave him clean clothes and pointed to a shower. "It was supposed to be for the officers. So, I got a fresh water shower. The other men took a salt-water shower." After showering, he slept while a meal was served. "It added up to be three days without eating. I don't remember what I ate that third day."

The destroyer took those rescued from the *San Juan* to the Fiji Islands. In the hospital for 10 days, Fischer's eyes were treated because of reactions to the crude oil. "One man went blind and three or four were sent home because of eye problems. I was lucky."

His family was informed of the Japanese attack. "The government sent a telegram to my folks that said I was slightly wounded." Fischer sent his own telegram asking them not to worry. A week later, a second telegram explained that Fischer was convalescing. A final telegram informed the family that Fischer had been released from the hospital.

The *San Juan* was carrying 1,464 men. The passengers included three units of the U.S. Army Air Corps — the 855th All Negro Engineers Battalion; the 253rd Ordnance Company; and the 1st Fighter Control Squadron, Fischer's unit. The 1st Fighter Control Squadron was comprised of 367 officers and enlisted men. Of the 117 men who died, Fischer said 13 were from his squadron. The *San Juan* stayed afloat for another two days after the Nov. 11 torpedo attack, sinking on Nov. 13. Fischer, and other men in the 1st Fighter Control Squadron received the Purple Heart. He thought it was six to eight months after the sinking of the *San Juan* and he was in the Philippines.

Two years before the attack, Fischer had been drafted into the Army Air Corps on Nov. 7, 1941. Twenty-one years old, he was living in California picking up odd jobs and hoping to get work at an aircraft factory. A month later, the Japanese bombed Pearl Harbor, bringing the U.S. into the war. He reported for basic training at Camp Roberts located midway between San Francisco and Los Angeles. Upon completion of basic training, he was stationed in Santa Maria, California, for 15 months. Fischer worked at a ham radio station used for West Coast defense. "I got paid $21 a month. That's what the government paid me, 69 cents a day."

It was Oct. 28, 1943, when Fischer and the 1st Fighter Control Squadron sailed from San Francisco on the *San Juan*. The ship was built in June and had made one round-trip passage to the South Pacific. Two weeks after its departure, the *San Juan* was torpedoed.

After recuperating on the Fiji Islands, Fischer and other survivors of the squadron were reunited for travel to Brisbane, Australia, where they arrived on Dec. 7, 1943. About three months in Brisbane was spent getting reorganized and re-equipped. "We lost everything on the *San Juan*."

Then began a series of island hopping where the unit stayed about two to three weeks on each island. Setting up at a base in the Philippines, Fischer sat at an Operations Board and tracked IFF (Identification, Friend or Foe). This was a secondary radar system that operated differently and independently of the primary radar system. The radar on the ground transmitted on one frequency and received a coded signal from the plane's transponder (transmitter-responder) on another frequency.

Men who were positioned at the Operations Board had been trained on radio and radar equipment. In the Philippines, they set up radio, cryptographic and radar connections between Allied land, air and sea forces. "There was a board with a map that was probably 10 feet by 10 feet." The Operations Board had random letters of the alphabet, like B, H and M. Fischer explained the letters didn't mean anything more than a plane had been spotted in that section. One of his jobs was to move a flag to the location where radar had determined a plane's location. "I had a long stick and could move the flags that I couldn't reach."

An officer was always at the Operations Board and it was his responsibility to make the decision if the plane was friend or foe. If determined the plane was foe, an alarm was sounded to shoot down that plane. Fischer doesn't know if a friendly plane was ever mistakenly shot down. Wearing earphones and always working with at least three or four other men, they each had 6-hour shifts before taking a break. Fischer explained planes returning from raids called using an IFF signal. "Then we knew they were friendly planes."

The first island-hopping stop was Wakde Island off the northern coast of New Guinea. On May 17, 1944, the Allies fought against almost 800 Japanese defending Wakde. "The Japanese planes would bomb us every night." During one move to an island close to the Philippines, Fischer said members of his squadron were on one of two ships moving together. A Japanese plane approached and released a torpedo that fell between the two ships. "Thank heavens. We were saved again."

Fischer said Japanese planes flew over every night while he was on islands around the Philippines. "We always hit the foxholes." Explaining he never had a weapon, he recalled being armed only during his basic training.

It was his last move that Fischer described with more emotion. Eight to 10 ships, including Merchant Marine ships, were moving in the Pacific. Fischer was on one of the Merchant Marine ships when a kamikaze (Japanese suicide pilot) bomber flew in and hit a ship. "That ship was behind our ship. There couldn't have been any survivors."

Describing another encounter with a kamikaze plane, Fischer said he knew it was after his ship. "He was so close, I could see the pilot." He credits a gunner on his ship for bringing that plane down just before it would have hit the ship. "That was the last of my scary moments being in the service."

Announcement of the war's end came while Fischer was on an island in the Philippines. He said there was no kind of celebration. "Oh yes, we talked about it. Naturally, we were all happy because the war was over. But we were getting moved from island to island all the time. Even when we got on a ship to go back home, it was just another move, get on another ship, head for home." On Nov. 5, 1945,

Fischer sent his parents in Washington County, Nebraska, another telegram. "Arrived in Frisco. Will be home soon." Also going home were two brothers, Eugene and Howard, who had served in the Army Air Corps.

From San Francisco, Fischer didn't get on another ship. First, he took a train to Omaha, then a train to Fremont and finally hitchhiked to Winslow. "Then I called home and someone came and got me. No more ships."

After the war, Fischer operated a road grader for the Washington County (Nebraska) Road Department. For 23 years, he worked on switching equipment for Great Plains Telephone in Blair, Nebraska. Fischer retired in 1985.

Ben Fischer lives in Fremont, Nebraska, and was married to Esther for 53 years. Their wedding date is July 25, 1957. They have 3 children, Curt, Joyce, and Gail; 2 grandchildren; and 4 great-grandchildren.

Warren Hammang
Army Air Corps

◇◇◇◇◇◇◇◇◇◇◇◇◇◇◇◇◇◇◇◇

Birth Date:
Nov. 10, 1925

Hometown:
Arlington, Neb.

Age When Enlisted:
18

Service Dates:
May 1944 –
May 1946

Highest Rank:
Staff Sergeant

Sometimes it's an embarrassing situation that will always be remembered. For Warren Hammang, 90, it happened in a brand new B-29 Superfortress bomber. The 11-man crew had enjoyed a night on the town in Emporia, Kansas, before the men prepared to leave for California.

Hammang explained it had been raining a lot in Emporia. The crew was preparing to leave Kansas the next morning. Not mentioning names, he related that the two waist gunners weren't paying attention. They were supposed to be watching the plane's wheels. "We were taxiing out to the main runway and got stuck in the mud. We had to get off the plane and stand at attention while the base commander chewed us out." A big earth-moving machine pulled the plane back on the runway. After it was checked for damage, the crew was given the OK to leave. "And, boy we got out of there," Hammang said, laughing.

In April 1943, Hammang and a friend, Calvin Menking, had enlisted in the Army Air Corps because they both wanted to be pilots. Only a junior in high school, Hammang had to wait a year. On May 13, 1944, he entered the service with two weeks left before his Arlington (Nebraska) High School graduation.

He reported to the Amarillo (Texas) Air Force Base for three months of basic training. Because he wasn't selected to be a pilot, Hammang was sent to Army Radio Technical Training School in Sioux Falls, South Dakota, to become a radio operator. The main emphasis was learning Morse Code, but the men also were instructed on how to identify aircraft and administer first aid.

During the seven months spent in Sioux Falls, the men stayed in barracks described as pared-down, tar-papered buildings designed for a warmer climate. The buildings had no insulation and one coal stove per barracks.

Sometimes it's a horrific eye-witness account that will always be remembered. In addition to radio operators, there were men in Sioux Falls training to fly planes. The twin-engine AT-18 held 18 students, the instructor, pilot and co-pilot. Waiting in their barracks before supper, the men "heard this plane just screaming and two of them had rammed together over the field," Hammang said. "One had chewed the tail off the other one and he just came straight down."

All 21 were killed in one plane. "The other plane lost an engine. We watched him climb on out and then the chutes started coming out. They all bailed." Nobody was killed in the second plane; it crashed somewhere over western South Dakota.

Leaving South Dakota for New Mexico (Clovis Army Air Field), 11-man crews were formed for the B-29 bombers. "We did a lot of flying out of there to get used to flying together."

Sometimes it's a funny scenario that will always be remembered. Training at Clovis included how to use a life vest. Hammang described a tall tower with a cable stretching over a swimming pool. The men jumped off the tower and held on to a pulley attached to the cable. "We would go roaring down and were supposed to wait until our feet were just about to touch the water." The next step was to release the life vest straps as the men hit the water. After pushing the release button, they would be free to swim. "You knew you were hitting something," Hammang said about the jolt upon first touching water. "Most of them went right to the bottom as soon as they hit the release button. Our pilot was a big tall guy and he hit the water and went right to the bottom," he added, chuckling.

Moving from the mud puddles of Kansas to the swimming pool of New Mexico, Hammang's crew finally made it to a large body of water — the Pacific Ocean. They landed at Mather Field (12 miles east of Sacramento, California) and spent one night while life rafts were loaded on the B-29 and the men were issued their life jackets.

Sometimes it's a name that's a tongue twister to pronounce that will always be remembered. One of the first stops for the B-29 crew outside the United States was Kwajalein (part of the Marshall Islands). "I don't know how to spell that," Hammang said, after pronouncing it three times. "It's just kind of a sandbar out in the middle of the Pacific Ocean. We probably stopped to just fuel up."

In July 1945, Hammang and the B-29 crew arrived at Guam. "That's when we were assigned to Tinian." One of the Northern Mariana Islands, Tinian is about 50 miles north of Guam and has a land area of 39 square miles. "It had six runways. That's where we'd be taking off to bomb Japan." As soon as the B-29 bomber crew members landed on Tinian, they lost their new aircraft. A crew with more seniority got the newer plane. "We got an old war-weary thing."

Describing his first of six missions, Hammang said they were trying to take out a naval base in Japan, probably in Osaka or Kobe. During every mission, Hammang said his position as radio operator could be "kind of a boring job." He explained when there was radio silence, he wasn't allowed to transmit once in a combat area because the Japanese would pick up everything. However, he was always wearing earphones and monitoring the receiver. All crew members wore coveralls, flak jackets, black helmets, life jackets and parachute harnesses. The parachute was on the floor close to their seats. "We got quite a bit of flak [anti-aircraft fire] on that first mission."

Never knowing the capacity of their bomb load, Hammang said the maximum was 10 tons. He also explained there could be up to 500 planes coming together from Guam, Saipan and Tinian for the bombing missions.

Hammang related that his B-29 crew didn't fly many high-altitude missions. "General Curtis LeMay was experimenting at going in at a lower altitude, as low as 5,000 feet. The Japs got a pretty good shot at you." However, there were advantages for the B-29 crew. "We had good accuracy and could carry more bomb load because we didn't have to climb way up there and that saved fuel. It took a lot of fuel to get up to 35,000 feet."

Pilots flying the single-seat P-51 Mustang provided protection for the B-29s. The P-51 was a long-range fighter designed for air-to-air combat and known for its speed, maneuverability and smaller size. "We had P-51s up there all the time. That was the best fighter that we had."

During one daylight mission, Hammang remembered the sounds. "You could hear the flak going off all around. Chunks of those shells hitting the side of the plane or hitting the wings. You'd hear a boom and then just like somebody threw a big handful of gravel against your plane."

Night missions were difficult because of the darkness. "You just tried to find a place that wasn't burning and then drop the bombs." Japanese fighters could fly above the B-29s, see their silhouettes over the burning fires and that created a perfect target.

Sometimes it's a close call that will always be remembered. On one night mission, the B-29 crew took off with 500-pound incendiary bombs (filled with magnesium) loaded in the bomb bay. An incendiary bomb was designed to set fire to objects as the result of a chemical reaction.

Propeller-like fuse spinners were attached to the bomb noses. When dropped, they whirled in the air and armed the bombs. A wire stuck through the propeller prevented it from spinning. "As long as they are hanging in the bomb bay, they're all right." Hammang explained when the door was opened to release the bombs, he watched the front bay to make sure they all fell out. George Braun, top gunner, watched the rear bay.

During this mission when the rear bomb bay door was opened, three of the bombs fell and jammed in the bottom of the bay. Braun saw what had happened and immediately ran to the bay. "He sat on the rack and put his feet in two of the propellers to stop them from turning. He held on with one arm and held the third propeller with the other arm."

One of the other gunners called over the intercom and Braun said he was in the bomb bay holding the propellers. The bombardier (crew member responsible for targeting aerial bombs) rushed to the bay. "He got ahold of the tail of the bomb some way or other and gave it a flip. And then all three of them fell out." After the propellers start spinning, a bomb will explode in 35 seconds. "It couldn't have been much time left. Braun was a hero."

When he wasn't flying a mission, Hammang said he slept a lot. He also was responsible for updating radio frequencies. "They were always changing frequencies on the transmitters."

Weather on Tinian also changed. Hammang said his sleeping quarters were in a Quonset hut. "The ground crews who worked on the planes lived in tents. There was a hurricane and all the tents were swept out to sea. Poor guys." The men crawled underneath the huts. "It was solid rain and wind and some of the Quonset huts were moving around." That's when the men crawled out from under the huts. "Seems to me we had to go down and sit in the planes and wait with the engines running into the wind to keep them from blowing away. The whole crew was in the plane."

Sometimes it's being somewhere when history is made that will always be remembered. On July 26, 1945, Hammang said the USS *Indianapolis* delivered to Tinian the atomic bomb that was dropped Aug. 6 on Hiroshima. "Nobody where we were knew anything about the bomb."

When Japan surrendered on Aug. 15, Hammang said he found out from MPs (military police). "We were all in bed sleeping because we'd had a 16-hour mission. The MPs came in and relieved us of our handguns and carbines." Other men who already heard the news were shooting their rifles in celebration. "They were running up and down the roads. They [the MPs] thought they'd better disarm everybody and then nobody would get shot."

Japan formally surrendered to the Allies on Sept. 2 in Tokyo Bay aboard the USS *Missouri*. "We were flying about

15,000 feet above the *Missouri* when they signed the treaty. There were lots of planes up there. You really didn't know whether the Japs were going to pull a fast one and attack the *Missouri*." Then Hammang added: "We weren't loaded. Just flying around and letting them know we were there."

The end of the war didn't mean Hammang was returning home. "I enlisted to a termination of the war plus six months." He said as "all the old timers" went home, those left pretty much had the island of Tinian to themselves.

Sometimes it's a real cold one that will always be remembered. After the war ended, those left on Tinian continued to get one bottle of beer a week. The men put their bottles in their barracks' bags. After maybe 12 men had accumulated a few beers, Hammang explained what happened next. "We had these big CO2 fire extinguishers on wheels. We'd take the nozzle and blow a bunch of that carbon dioxide in there. It would get real cold and we had to be careful so the bottles wouldn't freeze and break. Then we'd have a beer party."

Before returning to the U.S. in April 1946, Hammang was transferred to Clark Air Base in the Philippines where he worked in the mailroom. From there, he went to Honolulu, Hawaii, and then to Oakland, California. "It took nine days to get from Honolulu to Oakland. That was quite the trip."

One final train ride took him from Oakland to Fort Douglas in Salt Lake City, Utah, where he was formally discharged. One final trek took him home to Arlington,

Nebraska. "I hitchhiked home. In those days, if you were in uniform, they'd pick you up."

Sometimes it's something sad that will always be remembered. "My brother, Joe, was 16 years older than me. He was in the Army infantry, got shrapnel in his back and carried that to his grave. Joe had been home for about a year before me. He had post-traumatic stress disorder. He sat in the living room and looked at the wall for almost a year. There was no help."

Hammang also thought of his friend, Calvin Menking. The two enlisted together on April 24, 1943. Menking didn't come home. "He was a gunner and I heard that he was shot down on the third mission. Everybody in the front of the plane survived. The plane broke in two and the tail went down and he was in that end of it as a gunner."

Still, Hammang enjoyed being in the service. "I was kind of disappointed when it all came to an end." With no job opportunities when he got back to Arlington, he and a couple of friends bought a '41 Ford and took off for California.

Sometimes it's knowing the end of the story has a happy ending that will always be remembered. His California job involved travel. One assignment took him to the Canary Islands, where Hammang met Maria Bolanos Canino, and they have been happily married for 55 years.

After the war, Hammang worked 15 years for United Geophysical, a seismograph company in Pasadena, California. He traveled extensively and worked overseas, including Pakistan, the Persian Gulf, Venezuela, Colombia, Costa Rica, Argentina and the Canary Islands. Hammang retired in 1962.

Warren and Maria Hammang live in Fremont, Nebraska, and have been married for 55 years. Their wedding date is May 11, 1961. They have 2 sons, Sammy and Albert; and 2 grandsons.

Katheryn Howe
(Navy) WAVES

◇◇◇◇◇◇◇◇◇◇◇◇◇◇◇◇◇◇◇◇◇◇

Birth Date:
Oct. 31, 1921

Hometown:
Ewing, Neb.

Age When Enlisted:
23

Service Dates:
July 1944 –
April 1946

Highest Rank:
Pharmacist's Mate,
Second Class

At 61 inches tall, Katheryn Wood Howe, 94, met a requirement by an inch to enlist in the Navy WAVES (Women Accepted for Volunteer Emergency Service). She had to be 60 inches, or 5 feet.

In 1943, 23-year-old Howe read in the newspaper and heard radio updates about the war. She was working as a dental assistant in O'Neill, Nebraska, getting on-the-job training. But there was another constant reminder encouraging enlistment that kept drawing her attention. "I saw lots of posters." Some were for the WAVES: "Share the Deeds of Victory — Join the WAVES." "To Make Men Free 'you will share the gratitude of a nation when victory is ours.' Enlist in the WAVES

Today." Some were for the WAC (Women's Army Corps): "I'd rather be with them than waiting. The WAC, Women's Army Corps." "In the Victory to come . . . Here, too, will be the Honor and Glory. Good soldiers . . . The WAC."

Making the decision they both wanted to join the WAVES, Howe and her friend, Ruth Larson, drove to a recruiting office in Omaha, Nebraska. Just outside Omaha, Howe's car broke down. The two friends spent the night with Larson's relatives and the car got fixed. The next day at the recruiting office, Larson passed the physical and enlisted. "I didn't pass the physical. My mother said, 'You probably looked too bedraggled because of the car problems and then you became homesick.'"

Homesick? After Howe graduated from Chambers (Nebraska) High School at age 16, she received a scholarship to attend Grand Island (Nebraska) Business College. Grand Island was almost 100 miles from the family ranch outside Chambers. "I got homesick when I was there." Omaha was almost 200 miles from Chambers, so Howe admitted her mother was probably right and she was homesick.

For another year, Howe worked at the O'Neill dental office. Then one day she talked with WAC recruiters who were in town. "I just felt that I needed to enlist because I wanted to help in the war effort." Once again, she drove to Omaha; this time her destination was the WAC recruiting center. "I passed the physical and was accepted, but I didn't enlist." Homesick? "No, I still loved the Navy. Partly because of Ruth." Howe added with a laugh: "I liked the

WAVES uniforms the best. Those nice blues. The WACs had grey."

Her next step was to pass the WAVES physical, which she did. Howe enlisted on July 29, 1944, and remained stateside during her service. From a booklet describing the WAVES, Howe pointed to the back cover. "Serve your country in your country. Join the Navy WAVES. Release a Man to Fight at Sea."

Established by Congress as the women's branch of the United States Naval Reserve, the purpose of the WAVES was to release men for sea duty and replace them with women in shore stations. Signed into law by President Franklin D. Roosevelt on July 30, 1942, at least 75,000 women served in the WAVES during World War II.

In August 1944, Howe boarded a troop train in Omaha for the U.S. Naval Training Center at Hunter College near the Bronx in New York City. Fifty-five women spent six weeks living in dorms during boot camp. Learning Navy rules and regulations, studying ship-to-ship signals and doing lots of marching helped prevent Howe from getting really homesick. The women also experienced frequent, surprise inspections. "We had to keep our dorm room ship-shape. Whoever was inspecting would go over the windowsills looking for any dust. Of course, shoes had to be polished and uniforms had to be clean."

After boot camp, a long-term assignment was determined for each woman. "We had interviews about different qualifications and what we had done during private life. Because I had been a dental assistant, that's where they assigned me." At the time, the two largest naval hospitals were Bethesda Naval Hospital in Maryland and the U.S. Naval Hospital in San Diego, California. Howe was assigned to San Diego.

Not allowed to tell her parents she was leaving for California, Howe said her mother wasn't pleased. "Mother said, 'I won't tell anybody where you're going.' I knew something could slip out. Her intentions were good."

Understanding why she couldn't tell her parents where she would be stationed until she got there, Howe showed a picture of another poster. "If you tell where he's going … He may never get there!" The message was applicable to both naval men and women and was enforced for security reasons. Howe knew her mother was concerned, and she really appreciated her father's support. "He was perfectly willing for me to enlist. He wasn't in the service during World War I because his mother was an invalid and he helped on their ranch."

It was the next six weeks in San Diego where Howe came face-to-face with the harsh realities of the war. "I was assigned to dentistry in the hospital and this is where the bad things come in." Some patients could walk; others were carried on stretchers. These injured servicemen had endured days on hospital ships coming from the Pacific. "The broken jaws, the wired-up jaws, broken teeth." Howe's voice trailed off, "Those old bombs would hit."

Some of the men couldn't eat. Some could hardly talk.

"A lot of them recovered, but a lot of them didn't have full recoveries." After healing, some men required restorative work from, for example, loss of teeth or jaw injuries.

Although she worked only in dentistry, men treated for burns, head injuries and loss of limbs also were patients in the hospital. When some of the WAVES had free time, they visited men in other wards. "Because it was nice weather in San Diego, we would take outside some of the fellows who were beginning to recover. Two or three of us would push them in wheelchairs. The men liked to get out."

Also needing time away from the hospital, Howe got together with women she knew from Nebraska who were working in California as Rosie Riveters. A cultural icon, Rosie the Riveter represented American women who worked in factories and shipyards producing munitions and war supplies.

During her six weeks at the U.S. Naval Hospital in San Diego, Howe had quarters in a hospital room and also attended classes that focused on dental procedures. On Nov. 9, 1944, she completed a course of study as a General Dental Technologist.

Her last assignment duty was the U.S. Naval Air Station in Vero Beach, Florida. Traveling alone on a train, Howe stopped in Nebraska for a few days to see her parents for the first time since she left for boot camp about three months earlier.

Arriving in Vero Beach at night, there was no stationmaster on duty. She had no idea where the base was located and few people were at the railroad station. Then a couple of servicemen walked in. "I can't remember if they were sailors or Marines and both were on base." A brief conversation determined that all three were headed for the base. "They were walking and said I could walk with them." Guessing it was about a distance of 2 miles, Howe called the two servicemen nice, decent-looking guys. "Thank goodness for them. I don't know what I would have done."

The Vero Beach station became a night fighter training facility in December 1944. The Grumman Aircraft Engineering Corporation of Bethpage, New York, built one of the classic combat planes of World War II, the F6F Hellcat. From June 1942 to November 1945, Grumman produced 12,272 Hellcats, which was the largest number of fighter planes ever made in a single aircraft factory. Grumman delivered a Hellcat at the rate of one per hour around the clock. The first Hellcats saw action in the Pacific in September 1943.

When pilots were training, Howe said: "Once in a while a plane would go down and there might be an injury. But, I was seeing nothing like I did in San Diego."

She continued working as a dental assistant (pharmacist's mate) in the dispensary because there was no hospital at Vero Beach. The pharmacist's mate classification included women who worked in an actual pharmacy, as well as X-ray technicians, physical therapists, optician assistants, physician assistants and dental assistants.

No men injured during the war were brought to Vero Beach. Instead, those working on the base were seen for more routine dental procedures. About six assistants worked with three dentists. Howe cleaned teeth, mixed amalgam for silver fillings, developed X-rays and sterilized instruments.

During dental procedures on pilots, some of the WAVES hinted they sure would like a plane ride. Howe was one who hinted and subsequently got to fly over the Atlantic Ocean at night for about an hour. Landing smoothly on the runway, Howe related it was nothing like her first experience in an airplane. Her sister's boyfriend was the pilot and he scared her father's cattle while landing not very smoothly in a pasture.

Being away from the day-to-day treatment of injured servicemen in San Diego didn't mean Howe forgot about those servicemen. "There was nothing routine in San Diego. Every injury was different." Hearing the news on Sept. 2, 1945, that the war was over meant the constant influx of injured servicemen to hospitals also was over.

No more daily updates on the war. Instead, Howe was reading in the newspaper and hearing on the radio news about the end of the war. But it wasn't the end of her service commitment at Vero Beach. She was discharged on April 28, 1946. "Our base was closing and I was eligible to get out. Before I left from the dispensary, I think there was just me and another girl still there."

After being discharged in Miami, Howe took her last train ride as a WAVE back home to Nebraska. Her father met her in Omaha. Her mother was happy because she knew where her daughter was. As for Howe? "I'm glad I enlisted. Maybe I helped a little bit."

◇◇◇◇◇◇◇◇◇◇◇◇◇◇◇◇◇◇

After the war, Katheryn Wood attended Northwestern University Dental School in Chicago with financial support from the GI Bill and became a licensed dental hygienist in Illinois. While in Illinois, she became engaged to Wesley Howe, the Army truck driver with whom she had corresponded during the war. In 1949, Howe became the second licensed dental hygienist in Nebraska and she worked two years in the state. She then was a stay-at-home mother and also worked at Fremont Body & Frame, the Fremont business she and Wesley bought in 1965.

Katheryn and Wesley Howe live in Fremont, Nebraska, and were married for almost 68 years. (Katheryn died on Sept. 1, 2016.) Their wedding date is Oct. 10, 1948. They have 3 children, Peggy, Charles, and Mary Jo; and 2 step-grandchildren.

Wesley Howe
Army

◇◇◇◇◇◇◇◇◇◇◇◇◇◇◇◇◇◇◇◇◇◇◇

Birth Date:
Jan. 20, 1922

Hometown:
Chambers, Neb.

Age When Enlisted:
21

Service Dates:
February 1943 –
December 1945

Highest Rank:
T5 Corporal

How many parts does it take to assemble 104 new 1944 GMC Army cargo trucks on a beach in New Guinea? Wes Howe, 94, doesn't know either. But Howe, with the help of about 200 men in two Army companies, completed the assignment in a couple of weeks.

Parts for two weapons carriers (Dodge ¾ ton trucks) and four Ford GPWs (4-wheel drive utility vehicles similar to the Willys MB Jeep) also were packed in the crates. Were instruction manuals included? Howe laughed and said he didn't remember and he also didn't remember if there were leftover parts.

He did remember that in 1943 at truck school in Cheyenne, Wyoming, he had to take apart the motor of the same Army cargo truck and put it back together. But not the entire 6-cylinder, 6-wheel drive truck.

Howe was accustomed to driving a Farmall F-20 tractor and other farm equipment growing up on a ranch in Garfield County, Nebraska. His father died in 1941, leaving Howe, 19, at home with his mother and younger sister and in charge of over 300 head of livestock. The next year, the Howe family was confronted with a series of issues and decisions. Livestock and machinery were sold. The ranch was rented. Mother and sister got jobs at the Mead (Nebraska) Ordnance Plant. Howe enlisted in the Army on Feb. 17, 1943.

Basic training took him to Keesler Air Force Base in Biloxi, Mississippi. "There were so many men there, we lived out in the woods in squad tents with eight men to a tent."

Weather conditions included cold temperatures and rain. At the end of five weeks, many of the men were sick. "The sun would come out in the morning and we would collapse our tent around the pole. During the day it would rain again and everything would get wet." Why collapse the tent if it was going to rain later? "It was Army regulation. If the sun was out in the morning, the tents had to be collapsed."

After basic training, Howe was assigned as a truck driver and headed for additional instruction in Cheyenne for 3-4 months. Practicing how to travel in a convoy was a key aspect of instruction. A convoy is a group of vehicles traveling together for mutual support and protection. "We had to be a certain distance between trucks and try to maintain that distance."

Before Howe's company of about 100 men took a train to New Orleans, Louisiana, to leave the U.S., there was about a 6-month stay in Rapid City, South Dakota. This was the first place the men conducted target practice, using the semi-automatic, clip-fed M1 Garand rifle.

In New Orleans, the men knew they were going overseas; they just didn't know where. On its maiden voyage, Howe's naval transport ship, the SS *Sea Star*, passed through the Panama Canal on Christmas Day 1943. The men were promised a turkey dinner for the evening meal. "It took us all day to go through the Canal. Then we got out in the Pacific a ways and the ship went dead. We didn't have lights or nothing." Explaining the fate of the Christmas meal, Howe said: "Here we were trying to get served that turkey and it took all night. That turkey sat too long and pretty near everybody got sick."

A tugboat pulled the *Sea Star* into Balboa Harbor in Panama. "We were there maybe three weeks waiting to get the ship fixed." Operational again, the ship traveled with no escort. "At night we went around and around in circles. I suppose they did that in case there was a submarine somewhere."

Howe estimated it had been a week since the ship was towed to Panama for repairs. Then it happened again. "Way out there in the middle of nowhere and it went dead again. They didn't send out any tugs." Guessing the problem might have been the same as the first breakdown, ship personnel eventually got the ship moving.

The men finally knew their destination when the *Sea Star* docked in northern Australia at Townsville. "It took us 64 days!" Somewhat perturbed about the over 2-month travel time, it didn't help that the men had winter clothing with them. "Winter overshoes, winter coats, woolen stuff. We carried all that to Australia and then turned it in."

While in Australia, the troops weren't issued any equipment because this wasn't their final destination. "When we finally got orders to move, we went up to New Guinea, probably early March [1944]."

Since no trucks had accompanied the men when they left New Orleans, the vehicles were waiting in New Guinea — in those crates. The men set up poles and draped canvas for shade and began the assembly-line operation for putting the trucks together. "There were over 100 men in a company and we set up two companies. It amounted to 52 vehicles in each company."

The trucks were now drivable so the men could unload bombs and airplane fuel from ships in the harbor. If the water wasn't deep enough for a ship to come close to shore, a floating dock created access to the ship. Men drove the trucks onto the floating dock, and a boom with a long arm extension swung out for unloading the supplies.

Men also had the option of using a DUKW (D, designed in 1942; U, utility; K, all-wheel drive; W, dual rear axles), simply known as Duck. It served both as land and water transport.

After the bombs and fuel were loaded onto the trucks, they were unloaded at bomb dumps in the jungle. "We did a lot at night so nobody could see exactly where we were going." Howe explained that men on a work detail usually were at the dump site to handle the unloading. However, there were times when no one was at the bomb dump. "We dropped the tail gate of the truck, backed up and put the brakes on and that load of bombs would wind up in a pile out there and we'd take off." None of the bombs exploded. "The bombs have a cap on the end and the ordnancemen would put them on when loaded in the planes."

Because the fuel they were unloading was gasoline, truck and tractor tires were on the ground near the dump site. "We could put those rubber tires behind the truck and drop the containers of gasoline. It might put a dent in them, but they didn't break open."

Howe explained conditions faced. "It was pitch dark, and you didn't know who was out there. There were kamikazes [Japanese suicide pilots]. There were snipers. They'd hide out in the trees." Sometimes Japanese fighters got a direct hit on a jungle bomb dump. "That set off a heck of a fire. The only fire equipment over there was bulldozers. Covered the fire with dirt."

However, it wasn't dirt that was used for construction on New Guinea and other islands. Coral from the beaches created an excellent surface for runways. Howe explained when his company arrived in New Guinea, the island already had an airbase. B-24 bombers were flying out of Nadzab, and their targets probably were islands still controlled by the Japanese. "We'd operate for a few months and then move to the next one. As soon as the infantry and Marines invaded another island, we'd go in and get an airstrip going right away. We'd get a little closer to Japan all the time."

Coral was great for building airstrips but not for digging foxholes. "We slept in tents on the islands all the time." Blaring air-raid sirens frequently interrupted sleep. Sandbags piled high like an igloo served as some protection outside each tent. Search lights picked up Japanese incoming planes that Howe described as silver spots.

Eight men occupied a tent and, as squad leader, Howe said he hollered to alert his men and called out the men's names. "We could hear the planes coming even before the sirens went off." Men with large anti-aircraft guns on the ground began shooting. "That shrapnel would come back around and poke holes in your tent." The anti-aircraft guns were designed to attack aircraft and fire at high angles.

Between air raids and unloading ships, the men played baseball, softball and watched outdoor movies. Jack Benny and Carole Landis (American film and stage actress) were featured in one USO (United Service Organizations) show.

Howe also wrote letters to his mother and sister. His mother sent issues of the Chambers (Nebraska) Sun, his hometown newspaper. The editor listed in a special column men and women from the area who had enlisted or were drafted. If he recognized names in the articles, Howe wrote to them.

From New Guinea, Howe's company did a series of island hopping. The men moved to Morotai, a northern island of Indonesia. Next move was Mindanao, about 643 miles from Manila in the Philippines. Then the men stopped on Luzon, the largest island in the Philippines and finally sailed into Manila harbor.

"That harbor was so full of steel and ships and planes sticking out of it. They had a trail for us to follow to get in there. We sat there while they were evacuating prisoners. Then we operated out of Clark Field, a big airbase, for a long time." At Clark Field, the company received a second set of trucks — fully assembled.

Howe experienced a close call when he was unloading airplane fuel from a ship in Subic Bay, which is on the west coast of Luzon. "The ship was sitting back in the bay and there were all kinds of trees. A kamikaze came flying in and came over those trees and was headed for that ship." Men on the ground delivered anti-aircraft fire at the plane. "They cut loose on him. He was close enough to us he could have shot us with a pistol." After the plane took a hit, "It kind of slid off to the left and went into the bay and missed the ship by probably a block." Emphasizing what could have happened, Howe added, "That ship was loaded with 100 octane gas."

A series of very crucial events happened in 1945 while Howe was on another island, Ie Shima, located on the northwestern coast of Okinawa. The Battle at Okinawa was fought from April 1-June 22. Then the atomic bombs were dropped on Aug. 6 (Hiroshima) and Aug. 9 (Nagasaki).

"My company got orders and 23 of us were sent to Okinawa. The next morning we flew to Japan with instructions to go open an airstrip." It was Aug. 30. That 5-hour ride was memorable because the men flew in a C-54 transport. "Plush seats and everything. We weren't used to that. We traveled in old hot ships all the time."

Howe's company landed at Naval Air Facility Atsugi, a base about 25 miles from Tokyo, constructed by the Imperial Japanese Navy in 1939. Howe said the pilot gave the 23 men 15 minutes to unload the plane. "He just dumped us off. Afraid it might get sabotaged, I guess."

A U.S. serviceman arrived in a Japanese truck and drove the men to some Japanese barracks. "There was a little guard house and the old Japanese guard was standing there with his rifle and he bowed to us as we drove right past him." Most of the barracks were full of Japanese troops, but the Americans were able to find an empty one. "The first night or two we nailed windows shut. We didn't have any weapons, and there were 6,000 Japanese around with weapons."

The 23 men also didn't have any of their trucks. They were being sent by ship — again fully assembled — but didn't arrive for over a month. "We scrounged up all the old Japanese trucks we could get running."

Howe also stated that U.S. planes were starting to come in pretty fast with supplies, including freight and foodstuffs for Occupation troops that would be arriving. "With the help we had, we couldn't unload the planes that fast. So, we parked some of them on the dirt. Then it would rain and they were stuck in the mud."

The Japanese troops mostly stayed in their barracks. Until one day, Howe heard "clomp, clomp, clomp" and saw the Japanese men walking to a vacant field and tossing their rifles in a pile that Howe said became as high as a house.

When the formal peace treaty was signed on the USS *Missouri* in Tokyo Harbor on Sept. 2, Howe said his company was about a block from the ship. "We could see people walking around. There was a long table on the top deck."

In November, Howe left Japan for San Diego where he boarded a train to Fort Leavenworth, Kansas, where he was officially discharged from the Army on Dec. 19, 1945. "I got home just before Christmas."

A few months after his discharge, Howe began dating one of the hometown residents with whom he had exchanged letters while overseas. Katheryn Wood also was a veteran. She served for 21 months with the WAVES (Women Accepted for Volunteer Emergency Service, a unit of the U.S. Naval Reserve).

Wesley Howe, Army, and Katheryn Wood, Navy, married on Oct. 10, 1948. No regrets for a marriage that lasted almost 68 years. Any regrets for military service that lasted 34 months? Howe has severe hearing loss from the bombing raids and anti-aircraft barrage. Admitting there were a lot of tough days, he still said, "I would do it again."

◇◇◇◇◇◇◇◇◇◇◇◇◇◇◇◇◇◇◇◇◇◇◇

After the war, Howe worked at a Buick garage and a Ford dealership, both in Fremont, Nebraska. In 1965 he opened Fremont Body & Frame, where he worked for 32 years. He sold the business and retired in 1997.

Katheryn and Wesley Howe live in Fremont, Nebraska, and were married for almost 68 years. (Katheryn died on Sept. 1, 2016.) Their wedding date is Oct. 10, 1948. They have 3 children, Peggy, Charles, and Mary Jo; and 2 step-grandchildren.

Emery Johnson
Navy

◇◇◇◇◇◇◇◇◇◇◇◇◇◇◇◇◇◇◇

Birth Date:
June 21, 1924

Hometown:
Oakland, Neb.

Age When Drafted:
19

Service Dates:
June 1943 –
April 1946

Highest Rank:
Baker,
Third Class

As a baker in the Navy aboard the USS *White Plains* (CVE-66) (aircraft carrier, escort), Emery Johnson, 92, consulted a hand-written recipe book that called for mixing 18 pounds of flour, 18 pounds of lard, 1½ pounds of salt, 3½ pounds of sugar and cold water when he prepared to roll out 150 pie crusts.

When he was drafted as a 19-year-old, Johnson already had experience at a bakery. Oakland Bakery in his hometown of Oakland, Nebraska, employed him for two years. "While in high school, I worked at the bakery in Oakland. I used to go up there every night and make the dough for the next morning."

Before leaving his family in June 1943, Johnson emphasized the farthest he had been from Oakland was Lincoln (Nebraska), a distance of about 80 miles. His boot camp training took him to Farragut, Idaho, a distance of about 1,300 miles. "I was the most homesick boy you ever saw."

The train ride west included a stop at the North Platte (Nebraska) Canteen. "We got off for maybe a half hour. Everything was homemade — brownies, cakes, cookies. It was very good." The food rationing program in the U.S. began in spring 1942. With their stamps, citizens could buy limited amounts of items that included sugar and coffee. Volunteers donated their extra stamps so needed items could be purchased for the Canteen. After just over four years (Dec. 17, 1941 to April 1, 1946), 55,000 volunteers from 125 different towns had served troops that arrived on as many as 24 trains a day. Before his service ended, Johnson had two additional stops at the Canteen.

Johnson attended a church service during his first weekend away from home. "All the minister talked about was your loved ones at home. And by golly, I tell you, I was sick." Helping ease early homesickness were the letters from his parents and younger brother in Oakland. "And I was pretty good, too, at writing letters."

After boot camp, he traveled 375 miles west to Bremerton, Washington. The men waited in Bremerton for about a month where construction of the *White Plains* was nearing completion. The ship was commissioned on Nov. 15, 1943. About 2,000 sailors boarded the ship, and for the next 28 months the *White Plains* was Johnson's home. Knowing he would have a bed on the ship was one reason why Johnson chose to enlist with the Navy. "If you're in the Navy, you always have a place to sleep and shower. The Army men don't have that."

The ship's first voyage into the Pacific Theater was to the Gilbert Islands. The *White Plains* crew delivered aircraft to Tarawa Atoll in the Kiribati Islands (central Pacific Ocean) and then returned to Pearl Harbor. For the next few months, the crew conducted air operations and amphibious support training near Hawaii.

As a baker, Johnson worked with four or five other bakers. They were responsible for making only breads and desserts. His shift started at 3 a.m. and ended between 2-3 p.m. Also responsible for cleanup, Johnson washed a lot of pans. "We baked every day. Our schedule was a day on and a day off." On his days off, Johnson spent time on the flight deck watching the planes. As an aircraft carrier, the *White Plains* had a capacity for 28 planes, including dive bombers and fighter planes.

Johnson estimated about 20 sailors were responsible for preparing/cooking meals; others planned menus and ordered supplies. "We could go down to the coolers and get steaks. Everybody is your friend when you're in the cooking department because they want handouts. We ate good."

Bread was baked almost every day. "When we were ready to bake about 20 or so loaves of bread, one guy would weigh the dough on the scale and two of us would mold that into loaves." Noting how things change, he added, "I bet now they have something on the ships that makes the dough into loaves."

Serving 2,000 aboard ship meant basic dough for 400 buns had the ship's bakers using 60 pounds of flour. Chocolate cake called for 22 pounds of flour for 600 servings or 33 pounds for 900. Unquestionably, a lot of flour was needed daily and some got buggy before fresh supplies arrived. "When the guys would go through the chow line, they would hold the bread up to the light and if they saw black specks in there, that was bugs, so they wouldn't take it." Pausing for effect, and then laughing, Johnson added: "So, we started making dark bread. The bugs are still there, but they are cooked."

To avoid spoilage, powdered eggs and milk were used. "When we docked in the States, fresh milk would be brought back on ship. Then the men could have all the fresh milk they wanted."

Johnson said there never was a shortage of food on the *White Plains*. Even when the crew refused the buggy white bread, he didn't remember if the bread was thrown out. However, orange marmalade was tossed overboard. "We used to get it in cases and nobody would eat it. Guess they shouldn't have ordered it anymore."

Fresh supplies were unloaded while taking on fuel, which was a procedure called alongside connected replenishment. "We were always out to sea for a long time. The ship needed fuel and that's when they brought needed supplies." A supply ship pulled alongside the receiving ship in preparation for transferring fuel, fresh water, ammunition and bulk goods. The supplying ship held a steady course and speed, generally between 12 and 16 knots (14-18 miles per hour). The receiving ship moved alongside the supplier at a distance of approximately 30 yards.

Alongside connected replenishment was risky since the two ships moving side-by-side had to maintain the same speed and course for a long period of time. And, the hydrodynamics (dynamics of fluids in motion) of two ships moving closely together caused a suction between them. Any slight steering error could cause a collision or damage the fuel hoses and transfer lines.

San Diego was home port for the *White Plains*. The ship docked for maintenance but that was infrequent. "They put the ship in dry dock because that salt water is hard on it. So, they had to sand blast the bottom of the ship and then repaint it."

Sometimes taking a couple of weeks before the ship was seaworthy again, that's when the sailors had liberty. Noting the difference between liberty and leave, Johnson explained liberty meant the ship was anchored in a port and the men could go into town. "When you get leave, that is when you get to go home." While in San Diego, Johnson spent his days with five or six other sailors. "We were all too young and none of us could drink." Their routine was to eat at a cafe and afterwards go to a movie before heading back to the ship.

A couple times during liberty in San Diego, and also in Hawaii, Johnson saw his brother, Delwin, who was a

Navy pilot. "He knew when my ship was coming into harbor and that's how he got to see me." Delwin flew a dive bomber and took Johnson up for a ride a couple of times. Dean, the youngest Johnson brother, also was in the Navy and stationed in Bremerton, Washington. Ellery, the oldest brother, was a pilot in the Army Air Corps. Lois, sister of the Johnson brothers, married Charles McKee, who was in the Army. "And we all came home."

In October 1944, the *White Plains* was deployed to the Philippines. It was Oct. 25 when the general quarters emergency alarm sounded around 6 a.m. "All hands man your battle stations" quickly spread throughout the ship. "We fought the Japanese fleet in Leyte Gulf in the Philippines all day." Specifically, instructions for the men on board were to provide air support for the troops and also defend against submarine attacks.

The number of ships directly involved in the battle included: U.S., 216; Japan, 64; and Australia, 2. The *White Plains* took two direct kamikaze (Japanese suicide pilot) hits. "You could see daylight but it was above the water line. And it sprung the frame like you can spring the frame of a car." American losses totaled 1 light carrier, 2 escort carriers and 3 destroyers; the Japanese lost 26 warships. The Battle of Leyte Gulf (Oct. 23-25) was the largest naval battle of World War II and, according to some historians, the largest in history.

During this battle off Samar, Philippines, Johnson stayed in the bake shop across from the galley (kitchen) "because we had to send food and coffee up to those guys who were fighting with the guns all day."

Men who had a role in the Battle of Leyte Gulf received a Presidential Unit Citation dated Dec. 5, 1945. Admiral C.W. Nimitz, who commanded the Pacific Fleet during World War II, included the following paragraph as part of the Citation. "The Commander In Chief, U.S. Pacific Fleet, congratulates the officers, men and ships of this gallant task unit whose intrepid and heroic stand against a numerically superior and heavier enemy force in one of the most bitterly fought surface engagements of the war has added such an illustrious chapter to the history of the United States Navy."

After the Battle of Leyte Gulf, the *White Plains* returned to San Diego for repairs. During that time, the men had leave for a couple of months. When the *White Plains* was seaworthy again, the assignment for men on the ship was to participate in supportive rather than direct roles.

Almost 10 months after the battle in the Philippines, news of the Japanese surrender on Sept. 2, 1945, was delivered over the public address system. "It was a great day when that was announced." He was aboard the *White Plains*, but Johnson could be much more precise. "It's down in black and white and gives the location where we were out in the ocean." The Daily Plainsman was a newsletter printed on ship and distributed "when something important had to be told." Announcing the most important news since he had been aboard the *White Plains*, the next issue of the newsletter featured an article with the 3-inch high headline: WAR ENDS.

"At 1423 local time, the ship's position 24 degrees 26 minutes N. Lat., 150 degrees 24 minutes W. longitude, 1805 miles from San Diego, the captain made the following statement: 'The president at 1900 Eastern War Time, 1400 ship's time officially announced that Japan had surrendered unconditionally to the Allied nations, the United States, Great Britain, Russia and China. General MacArthur has been appointed supreme allied commander in the Pacific. Formal signing of the surrender is expected to take place as soon as arrangements can be made.'"

The Daily Plainsman also included an article on a new draft regulation from Willie M. Dickey, Commander, USN executive officer. "The President made the following statement tonight: 'The war department has recommended and I have approved, a request to the director of selective service to reduce inductions immediately from 80,000 to 50,000 per month. This figure will provide only sufficient men to support the forces required for occupation duty and to permit the relief of long service men overseas to the maximum extent transportation makes possible. In justice to the millions of men who have given long and faithful service under the difficult and hazardous conditions of the Pacific War and elsewhere overseas a constant flow of replacements to the occupational forces is thought to be imperative. Mathematically and morally no other course of action appears acceptable. Transportation by air and sea should make possible the release from the Army of five to five and a half million men during the next twelve to eighteen months.'"

Arrangements were made to have bunks welded on the hangar deck of the *White Plains*. The ship made stops at Pacific islands to transport men with enough points for discharge back to San Diego. Referring to meals served on the ship, Johnson said, "Those Army guys thought we Navy men really ate good."

Johnson did not have enough points for discharge immediately after the war ended. He referred to low-point men and high-point men. "You had points to get out. So many points for your age, so many points for sea duty, so many points for how long you were in the service. I can't remember what the number was, but I used to figure mine up every day." The *White Plains* traveled to Panama and back to Boston, Massachusetts, both places where the men had liberty. "We were just loafing." He was discharged on April 6, 1946.

Walking off the *White Plains* for the last time, Johnson said it was "just like leaving home. My service time was just about three years, but I had been on the ship for 28 months." The ship was decommissioned on July 10, 1946. "I think it was cut up and went to the junkyard."

Back home in Oakland, Johnson would have to cut the ingredients in his recipes by a lot if he got the urge to bake. After all, when he made the pumpkin pie filling for those 150 pie crusts on the *White Plains*, Johnson followed a recipe calling for 80 pounds of pumpkin, 8 dozen eggs, 12 ounces salt, 2 ounces cinnamon, 2 ounces mace, ½ ounce allspice, 2 ounces cloves, 24 pounds sugar and 6 to 7 gallons milk and water.

◇◇◇◇◇◇◇◇◇◇◇◇◇◇◇◇◇◇◇◇◇◇

After the war, Johnson was employed at Backstrom Grocery in Oakland, Nebraska. In 1952, he began his job in line maintenance for Northern Natural Gas Company in Nebraska (Oakland and Hooper). Through a merger, Northern Natural became Enron. After 30 years, Johnson retired from Enron in 1983.

Emery and Mary Johnson live in Fremont, Nebraska, and have been married for 67 years. Their wedding date is Aug. 5, 1949. They have 2 children, Jerry and Kathy; 4 grandchildren; and 4 great-grandchildren.

Marie Johnson
Army Nurse Corps

◇◇◇◇◇◇◇◇◇◇◇◇◇◇◇◇◇◇◇◇◇

Birth Date:
Sept. 5, 1922

Hometown:
Octavia, Neb.

Age When Enlisted:
22

Service Dates:
May 1944 -
May 1946

Highest Rank:
First Lieutenant

Before Marie Kopecky Johnson, 94, arrived in Guam as an Army nurse who treated men injured in combat, she encountered her own combat in the Pacific Ocean. Typhoon. Although she wasn't afraid of the water, she didn't know how to swim.

On board a hospital ship late in 1944, Johnson explained how the ship kept rocking back and forth. "Everyone was so sick and no one could even get out of bed." No one except for two nurses. "She and I were trying to take care of everybody who was vomiting." At one point, the two even went to find something to eat. "I had a good stomach," Johnson said, laughing.

Prior to her Guam arrival, Johnson enlisted in the Army Nurse Corps on

May 13, 1944. The attack on Pearl Harbor (Dec. 7, 1941) occurred during her first year at St. Catherine's School of Nursing in Omaha, Nebraska. "Hearing about the war helps draw you to join. Women also were being encouraged to go into the service, so my roommate during nurses' training and I decided to go." She graduated from St. Catherine's in 1943, passed the state nursing boards in spring 1944 and received her degree as a registered nurse.

Before she enlisted at age 21, Johnson didn't talk about the decision with her parents, who farmed outside Octavia, Nebraska. Her older brother, Rudy, was already serving in the Army infantry in Germany. "Now, I think back about how my mom must have felt with a son already in the war and now her daughter also was going."

The United States Congress authorized establishment of the Army Nurse Corps on Feb. 2, 1901. At the onset of World War II, fewer than 7,000 women were in the Corps. By the end of the war, more than 59,000 American nurses had served. Their efforts contributed to the statistic that fewer than 4 percent of American servicemen who received medical care in the field or underwent evacuation died from wounds or disease.

Johnson enlisted at Fort Crook outside Omaha and took a troop train to Santa Ana Army Air Base (about 33 miles southeast of Los Angeles) in California for four weeks of basic training. In addition to learning about Army organization and military regulations, the nurses also received training in field sanitation and defense against air, chemical and mechanized attack. From July 1943 through September 1945, approximately 27,330 newly inducted nurses graduated from 15 Army training centers.

After basic training, Johnson was sent 450 miles northwest to DeWitt General Hospital in Auburn, California. DeWitt opened in February 1944 specifically to receive and treat war casualties. Working 12-hour shifts, Johnson said the hospital generally was at capacity with injured men coming from overseas. "I knew what had to be done and just did it."

Her next assignment was Guam and she boarded the USAHS (United States Army Hospital Ship) *St. Mihiel.* On the return trip, the ship carried injured men who would be hospitalized in the United States. Protected by the Geneva Convention, hospital ships could only be used for medical purposes and were manned by civilian crews. Most were converted passenger liners and cargo or troop ships. They were forbidden to carry cargo of any kind and were subject to enemy inspection at any time. Painted mostly white, the ships were to be unarmed and marked with the red Geneva Cross.

When the war ended, 24 Army-authorized hospital ships were in service, having treated 16,755 patients. In addition, the Navy added another 15 ships. Each was standardized to carry one medical officer, one dental officer and 15 emergency management personnel to care for 100 patients.

Just a few days en route to Guam, the typhoon hit. Lasting 2-3 days, it made the 2-3 week passage seem longer, Johnson said. Arriving on the island and being once again on solid ground was bittersweet. "I remember thinking there isn't anything here." There was an airstrip, there was a place set up for the hospital and there were barracks with cots. "We worked every day in 12-hour shifts, which was just fine with us since there wasn't anything else to do."

Johnson said injured men were continually being brought to the hospital. Not sure how many doctors and nurses worked at the hospital, she mentioned corpsmen were available to help. Navy corpsmen were enlisted medical personnel who were regular combat troops except they carried medical supplies. Because Japanese fighters could be hiding in the jungle, two corpsmen served as escorts when the nurses made rounds.

Inside the hospital, a large tent-like structure with many cots, the area was divided into injury categories. Johnson worked with men suffering from severe burns. "It was really bad. They really suffered because back then we just didn't have the treatments that they have now." Grateful for what they did have, there always seemed to be sufficient medical supplies. In an effort to keep bandages clean and sterile, they arrived individually wrapped in crates.

Before burned skin areas were treated with ointments and wrapped in gauze, the men were given shots for the pain. When the bandages were changed, skin was pulled off with the gauze. "I remember the guys would just scream from the pain."

During Johnson's assignment on Guam, the nurses never ate alone. "These little lizards were everywhere.

When we were eating, they just climbed up and helped themselves." The reptiles even made themselves at home in the tents and skittered across the cots.

In addition to the constant presence of lizards on the island, it rained frequently. "At least four or five times a day. When it stopped, it was just a short break." Johnson said there wasn't the smell of fresh air after it rained. "I thought it made the entire island smell like mildew." Lots of rain meant lots of mud. The nurses wore tan boots with their khaki-colored dresses. "We had slacks but usually wore the Army Nurse Corps dresses."

After six months in Guam and the surrender of Japan on Sept. 2, 1945, Johnson was assigned to the 27th General Hospital in Tokyo, which had originally been a hotel. Two things about the hospital water were unforgettable for Johnson. She couldn't drink it and she never had a hot shower. "One of the things they kept stressing to us when we got there was that we absolutely could not drink water out of any faucets. Back in the U.S., it took me a while before I would drink from a faucet."

The nurses had sleeping quarters on a designated hospital floor. "It was a large room with Army cots." There were no lizards, but the nurses were awakened frequently from earthquake tremors. "They weren't severe enough to knock things over and we just got used to them."

Although the nurses were still working 12-hour shifts every day, Tokyo offered breaks from the daily routines they had endured in Guam. One diversion involved five nurses and a Tokyo train conductor. The nurses had been told they were not to leave the hospital without an escort or use any means of Japanese transportation. Curious about downtown Tokyo, one day Johnson and four other nurses disregarded both orders. They walked the short distance from the hospital to the train station and climbed in the front train car. The conductor excitedly exclaimed: "No, no no. You can't get on here." The nurses responded, "Yes, yes, yes." The next action spoke louder than words when the conductor got up and pushed the five women off the train. Laughing as she told what happened next, Johnson said, "We all rolled down a hill and nobody got hurt." Everybody had a good laugh. Back at the hospital, there were no ensuing consequences. "I think they were just glad we got back so we could get back to work."

One final Tokyo adventure for Johnson was when a pilot friend offered to take her for a ride. "Little did I know his plan was to buzz Tokyo upside down in that plane! It's a wonder I didn't fall out because there were no seat belts." The laughs after the aborted train ride and the elation of landing safely on the ground after the harrowing plane ride, Johnson said, were experiences that provided welcome relief from her duties of taking care of severely burned servicemen.

After six months in Tokyo, Johnson returned to the U.S. on a full troop ship sailing for Seattle. Being overseas for more than a year, she was eager to get home. "It was a long sail and I was so excited to get back to the United

States." Just as the typhoon lengthened her arrival in Guam, a different delay lengthened her arrival home. Nearing Seattle, the passengers got the news that no one would be disembarking and the ship would be quarantined for about two weeks. During the quarantine period, Johnson played Solitaire. "I had a little deck of cards with me overseas and I still have it." Never learning why the ship was quarantined, passengers were only told someone had a disease. During the delay, boats delivered fresh milk and ice cream that Johnson said was a real treat.

Finally on land, Johnson boarded a train for Fort Sheridan in Illinois, where she was discharged on May 13, 1946, exactly two years from her enlistment date of May 13, 1944. Everyone on the troop ship who landed in Seattle went to Fort Sheridan to be discharged. That meant there were lots of people, lots of lines, and once again, lots of time to play Solitaire.

Back home in Octavia was brother Rudy, who had been discharged earlier. The family was together again and, most importantly, both brother and sister had made it home safely.

Johnson summarized her feelings about being in the Army Nurse Corps: "Having a strong faith and depending on prayers to get through another day helped while I served during World War II. I did the best I could and it's something I'll never forget. I'm glad I did it."

◇◇◇◇◇◇◇◇◇◇◇◇◇◇◇◇◇◇

After the war, Johnson worked at the Schuyler (Nebraska) Hospital. In 1950, Marie and Harry (her husband) opened Johnson Farm Equipment Company in North Bend, Nebraska. She was bookkeeper and also conducted sales transactions until she retired in 2013.

Marie Johnson lives in Fremont, Nebraska, and was married to Harry for 32 years. Their wedding date is Nov. 11, 1948. They have 4 children, Galen, Rodney, Thomas, and Rita; 15 grandchildren; 17 great-grandchildren; and 1 great-great-grandchild.

Robert Kroenke
Navy

◇◇◇◇◇◇◇◇◇◇◇◇◇◇◇◇◇◇◇◇◇◇

Birth Date:
May 15, 1927

Hometown:
Dodge, Neb.

Age When Enlisted:
18

Service Dates:
May 1945 –
September 1949

Highest Rank:
Petty Officer,
First Class

Approximately 3,500 men on a small naval carrier getting paid monthly. Who handles that payroll and what are the logistics? Bob Kroenke, 89, was a Navy Disbursing Officer for over two years on the USS *Palau* (CVE-122) (aircraft carrier, escort).

"There were just three of us in the disbursement office." Once a month on payday, those three men set up tables. Men on board presented a slip to Kroenke's assistant. He found the names, checked them off and gave the slip to Kroenke. Estimating the average monthly pay for the men on the *Palau* was $150, Kroenke said they were paid in cash. "We paid out a lot of two dollar bills." Being responsible for all that money meant Kroenke and a first lieutenant went ashore when the ship was in port "with our 45s to bring back thousands and thousands of dollars."

Those aboard the *Palau* indicated on the slip of paper how much of their pay they wanted in cash. Like Kroenke, maybe they sent some money home to family. "Since there were five other kids at home when I was in the service, and sometimes Dad didn't have very good crops, I would make out an allotment for a few months." He sent his parents living on a farm outside Dodge, Nebraska, about $30 during each of those months. Kroenke said his monthly pay was maybe $100 or $120. At Christmas, the money bought presents for the family of seven. "One time Dad said toward March he bought some pigs."

Referring to a roster that indicated the amount of pay due each man, Kroenke kept records of what was distributed each month and what was carried over to the next month. Every financial transaction involved completion of paperwork. An accurate accounting was necessary to keep track of how much money each man kept and how much should be sent home to family.

He also kept records regarding amounts deducted for allotments like savings account deposits or war bonds purchase. A $25 war bond cost $18.75 and could be redeemed for the face value 10 years after purchase. By the end of his service, Kroenke had purchased 48 bonds.

The Bureau of Naval Personnel in Washington D.C. required a completed roster every month, indicating how much money each man on board had coming and what he actually drew. "It was my job to make out this roster. And this had to be typed perfectly. No strikeovers. I was using manual typewriters and calculators." Once the payroll was distributed, the entire process began for the next month. "I was figuring pay continuously."

When Kroenke enlisted in April 1945, he didn't immediately begin working in disbursement. First, he was 18 years old and still a senior in high school. He and his father rode from Dodge with a trucker who was driving a load of cattle to the Omaha (Nebraska) Stockyards. From there, they took a cab to the recruiting center in downtown Omaha.

Kroenke chose the Navy because he respected an uncle who had spent eight years in the Navy. After his father signed papers giving Kroenke permission to enlist, an important question had to be answered. "I wanted to finish high school and I asked if they would let me." That request was granted and he returned home to finish his senior year of high school.

On May 11, Kroenke was on his way to boot camp at Naval Station Great Lakes in Illinois for 12-13 weeks. Like many other 18 year olds, he had never been out of Nebraska. "Joining the Navy, things were done in order." That meant getting up, eating breakfast, marching drills and practicing at the rifle range. Just before his arrival in Illinois, Germany surrendered on May 7, 1945.

A troop train from Illinois headed west and Kroenke received additional training in San Bruno, California. A scheduled stop was the North Platte (Nebraska) Canteen. From Dec. 17, 1941, until April 1, 1946, a total of more than six million servicemen and women were served sandwiches, cakes, cookies, fruit and other special treats. The North Platte Canteen is recognized as one of the largest volunteer efforts during the war. The reason so many trains carrying servicemen stopped in North Platte is because the city was designated as a service point for Union Pacific Railroad. The train crews lubricated the wheels and topped off water levels in the tanks for the steam locomotive. Allowed to get off the train, Kroenke said it was a unique experience. "We all piled out and there were quite a few of us on this troop train. All these ladies met us with sandwiches and more."

The train arrived in San Bruno, where the men traveled to an old racetrack converted to a training camp. About 100 men received amphibious training that included instruction on the Higgins boat. Kroenke knew Andrew Jackson Higgins was born in Columbus, Nebraska, and was well known for designing and producing the LCVP (Land Craft, Vehicle, Personnel) boat. Usually just called the Higgins boat, its distinctive feature was a bow that dropped to become a front ramp. This design meant men and equipment were transported to shore, which eliminated the need for established harbors. President Dwight E. Eisenhower said in 1964: "Andrew Higgins is the man who won the war for us. If Higgins had not designed and built those LCVPs, we never could have landed over an open beach. The whole strategy of the war would have been different." Kroenke explained the Higgins boats hung on the side of the ship like a lifeboat and access was with a ladder. Training at San Bruno included always making sure the boats "were in shipshape order."

After a little over two months at San Bruno, Kroenke was transferred to Hunters Point close to San Francisco. He boarded the USS *Bergen* (APA-150) (auxiliary, personnel, attack). "We headed out to the Philippines. I think the bomb was dropped when I was in San Bruno, but the ship's orders were to be followed. There was no change because it wasn't sure what was going to happen after the bomb was dropped." The atomic bomb was dropped on Hiroshima on Aug. 6, 1945.

On the *Bergen*, Kroenke was a boatswain's mate, which meant his duties included maintenance and upkeep of the ship's structure and equipment. With about 300 men on board, the *Bergen* first stopped in Subic Bay, Philippines, before proceeding to Manila. "There were ships that had been sunk in the harbor. It was a mess."

Dropping the atomic bomb on Hiroshima and on Nagasaki (Aug. 9, 1945) altered where Kroenke would go next. Instead of heading to Japan, the *Bergen* stayed in the Philippines and stopped for men (Manila and Subic Bay) who had enough points to earn their military discharge. "We were picking up the enlisted men who were probably coming from various islands in the South Pacific. We picked up Army and Navy personnel to bring them back to San Diego. I think we had maybe 200 people."

The *Bergen* wasn't a transport ship and only had sufficient bunks for its crew. "We were in close quarters. But, they wanted to get home and were willing to do anything to get there." That meant sleeping wherever the men found space and using their duffle bags and sea bags as pillows. Upon arrival in San Diego, Kroenke wasn't going home. The *Bergen* headed for Norfolk, Virginia, where it was decommissioned, and he was transferred to the USS *Roosevelt* (CVB) (aircraft carrier, large).

On the *Roosevelt*, Kroenke thought the crew was close to 4,500 men. He helped maintain 40 mm guns. Other duties included fueling and cleaning airplanes. The ship conducted maneuvers as part of a fleet in the Atlantic Ocean. "We were close to the equator but never crossed it." He estimated the fleet included 10 to 15 battleships, cruisers and destroyers that specifically were protecting the *Roosevelt*, the only aircraft carrier in the fleet. "I can even remember one time we were in the Atlantic Ocean and [President] Harry Truman came aboard our ship and went out for maneuvers. I saw him at a distance." Planes frequently took off and landed on the deck of the *Roosevelt*. "One of my disabilities is hearing. When they shot those planes off the ship's deck there's a terrible noise."

After about two months on the *Roosevelt*, Kroenke saw a notice in the ship's bulletin announcing an open position in the disbursement office. He applied for, got the job and worked in that office for about four months before assuming the same position on the *Palau*. The *Roosevelt* was going to be docked in Norfolk, Virginia, and the *Palau* was heading for the Mediterranean. "I said that sounds better to me than sitting in Norfolk. So, I volunteered. They say you should never volunteer, but I did." While in Norfolk waiting for the *Palau* to leave port, Kroenke said he enjoyed eating seafood because, ironically, he never got any while aboard ship.

It was June 1947 and Kroenke remained on the *Palau* until Sept. 30, 1949, when his service ended. While on leave earlier in September, he enrolled at the University of Nebraska (Lincoln). "Now I'm going to have to miss two weeks to go back to Norfolk [Virginia] to get my discharge." Just like the Navy waited a couple of weeks until Kroenke finished high school, his professors waited a couple of weeks until he returned from Virginia.

Kroenke appreciated being able to use the GI Bill when he earned both bachelor's and master's degrees at the University of Nebraska. Having lots of experience counting money as a disbursing officer in the Navy, he did not earn degrees in accounting. However, numbers were just as important teaching students in Industrial Arts classes. "Measure twice; cut once."

After the war, Kroenke taught high school Industrial Arts classes for 35 years, retiring in 1989. Thirty-three of those years were at Fremont (Nebraska) High School. When Bob and Mary Lou, his wife, bought their Fremont house in 1957, they cashed in the 48 war bonds. The $1,200 was used for the down payment on their house.

Bob Kroenke lives in Fremont, Nebraska, and has been married to Mary Lou for 65 years. Their wedding date is June 11, 1951. They have 2 sons, Steve and Tom; and 1 grandson.

Lyle Martin
Navy

◇◇◇◇◇◇◇◇◇◇◇◇◇◇◇◇◇◇◇◇◇◇◇

Birth Date:
Dec. 19, 1924

Hometown:
Walthill, Neb.

Age When Enlisted:
18

Service Dates:
June 1943 –
April 1946

Highest Rank:
Aviation Ordnance-
man, Third Class

As an aviation ordnanceman, Lyle Martin, 91, was a weapons specialist in charge of storing, servicing, inspecting and handling weapons and ammunition carried on naval aircraft. He worked with machine guns and bombs.

However, when Martin trained with weapons during boot camp at Farragut Naval Training Station in Bayview, Idaho, he practiced with wooden rifles. "They didn't have enough rifles at that time to go around. So, they made these wooden rifles for the recruits that looked exactly like a regular rifle." He was quick to add that there was a rifle range where his platoon had target practice and used real rifles with real bullets.

At Farragut, seven camps occupied the base

and each camp had its own company of about 100 men. Two platoons comprised a company. "We had to lie down, sit up, stand up and fire five shots each time." Was he a pretty good marksman? "Well, I passed it. I had done a lot of hunting growing up on a farm outside Macy, Nebraska."

After the bombing of Pearl Harbor on Dec. 7, 1941, Martin knew he would join the military. "That was the thing to do at the time. Everybody was joining." That included Martin's older brother, Kenton (Navy), and younger brother, Melvin (Army). Kenton was on Merchant Marine ships that transported troops. Melvin entered the service just at the end of the war. In 1941, Martin still had two years of high school ahead of him. Two years later, he was 18 and graduated from Macy High School. His senior classmates included four boys and one girl. Martin wanted to join the Marines, so he traveled the 80 miles from Macy to Omaha, Nebraska. Because he was draft age, Martin was told to return home, wait to be drafted "and they would decide which branch I would be in."

Leaving the Marines recruiting station, Martin saw the Navy recruiting station was next door. "I walked in there and they told me the same thing." A man working there, however, was from Macy. "He told me to go back and have them put my name on the next month's list. When I got the notice, I was to let him know and he would send me a letter of recommendation for the Navy." The next time he traveled to downtown Omaha was for his physical and Martin had his letter of recommendation. He enlisted in the Navy on June 30, 1943.

On a train to Farragut Naval Training Station, the conductor told the men several miles before North Platte, Nebraska, "You guys are in for a treat." The train stopped at the North Platte Canteen and the treats included sandwiches, hard boiled eggs, doughnuts and cake. Anybody who had a birthday on the day the train stopped at the Canteen got a special cake, many times angel food. It's estimated about 20 birthday cakes were presented each day. During his almost three years in the Navy, Martin was on a train that stopped in North Platte four times for about 15-20 minutes during each stop. Once the men were not allowed off the train and high school girls and women handed boxes of food through the windows.

Leaving the Canteen, the men still had over 1,000 miles on the train before arriving at Farragut. About 15 months before Martin enlisted, ground was broken in March 1942 for the Farragut Naval Training Station. By September 1942, the base had a population of 55,000. Sailors receiving boot camp training at Farragut totaled over 293,000. After 30 months, the facility was decommissioned in June 1946.

Upon arrival at Farragut, the sailors reported for haircuts. "The whole platoon of us marched in there to get our hair cut and there were about eight or ten chairs and only two barbers." The first six men in line were told to stand by a chair and start cutting hair. Martin said they responded, "We don't know how to cut hair." The response to their concern was straightforward. "You don't need to. You just follow their head." Martin added, "It was quite the deal because everybody was hollering and yelling, 'Don't cut this and don't cut that.'"

After all the men received their short haircuts, they participated in one boot camp training activity at Lake Pend Oreille. "We had to jump in the lake and stay afloat for five minutes. I knew how to swim, but five minutes is quite a while to say afloat." The men also learned how to use their jeans as a life preserver. "You took your jeans and tied the legs in a knot and threw them over your head to get air in them. That, and your white cap, was supposed to help you stay afloat for a little while."

Reflecting on his eight weeks of training at Farragut, Martin said: "Eight weeks of training; it's a wonder we won the war. They took a whole bunch of green city and country kids and gave them eight weeks of training and then put them out there against the German and Japanese soldiers. That's the reason, I think, we lost so many. Besides that, the leaders had never been in war either. They were training more or less with the rest of us. There were a lot of mistakes made."

From Farragut, Martin was sent to Norman, Oklahoma, for Aviation Ordnance School. For 10 weeks, about 50 men in his company received training on the .30-caliber and .50-caliber machine guns. Martin didn't wear ear protection and he has severe hearing loss in one ear. "It wasn't even mentioned. I didn't go to the doctor because I would have been kicked out of the Navy." Martin practiced shooting and learned to boresight, which was a method of adjustment to pre-align the sights. If a gun malfunctioned, he had to make repairs. "The .50-caliber would fire once or twice but usually didn't fire the 10 rounds that was in it. We had to field strip it and figure out what was wrong and repair it quickly."

Field stripping meant no tools were used. Martin explained: "You take the barrel out, and when you put it back in, it has to line up correctly. Depending on which side the ammunition was coming into the machine gun, there was a switch there and you had to make sure it was set to where it was coming in from this side or coming in from the other side." This had to be completed within 2 minutes.

Two machine guns were mounted on each airplane wing and two on the fuselage that would fire past the plane's propeller. The guns on the fuselage were on a cam. When the propeller got so far, then the gun would fire. "By the time the bullet got there, then the prop was past. The bomb nosecone had a propeller and it had to turn so many times in order to line up to get to a firing line. If it didn't, it dropped as a dud."

Inside the plane, the bombs were loaded in racks and shackles. "The firing pin had to be set, usually before they were loaded onto the plane. So they were armed and ready to go."

After his 10 weeks at Aviation Ordnance School in Oklahoma was completed, Martin was sent to Alameda Naval Air Station in California for about a year. His duties there included "a lot of sentry/guard duty." However, he still worked with weapons. "I loaded ammunition belts for .30- and .50-caliber guns." Each belt had several hundred cartridges; the .50-caliber could fire 850 rounds a minute. Rounds were inserted manually into an ammunition belt. The belt was then lapped back and forth and inserted into a steel box.

In June 1945, Martin arrived at his final base assignment on Ford Island, about 30 minutes from Honolulu, Hawaii. Initially, he and two other men were told they were going to Leyte Island in the Philippines. "When we docked in Hawaii, two of us were told to get our gear because we were staying here." No explanation was given and Martin stayed until the end of the war.

Continuing to work with ordnance, Martin spent a lot of time reloading ammunition. "And, when carriers came in after being hit by kamikazes [Japanese suicide pilots], we took bombs and ammunition off of them." Although he couldn't remember the name of one specific ship, it remained fresh in his mind. "The kamikaze had hit the side of the carrier and went into the hangar deck and exploded. There was another hole out the other side of the ship. There were lots of fatalities." The munitions that already were defused had to be taken off that carrier and taken to the bomb farm. Martin described the bomb farm as being like a park with igloo-like structures covered with grass and trees growing around them for camouflage. The carrier returned to a port for repairs. Martin said it was the most damage that he saw while in Hawaii. Lesser damage occurred to a ship's superstructure (parts of the ship built above the hull and main deck) when enemy fire hit the deck.

Ford Island had been the epicenter of the Japanese attack on Pearl Harbor on Dec. 7, 1941. Evidence of the attack was still obvious 3½ years later. When Martin had liberty (permission to leave the base), he had to take a ferry for a 30-minute ride to Honolulu. "The sunken Arizona was right there where we boarded the ferry and we could see the oil coming up. We could see some of the superstructure and it was still leaking oil."

About two months after his arrival in Hawaii, Japan surrendered on Sept. 2, 1945. Martin remembered exactly where he was that day. "I was in Honolulu buying an engagement ring. It took me three hours to get back to Ford Island. Everything was bazookey. Everyone was running all over the place and hollering and yelling."

Although it took Martin a little over seven months after the end of the war to accumulate enough points to be discharged, he didn't keep the engagement ring with him. He had bought the ring for a girl he met two years ear- lier (Sept. 11, 1943) on his last night of boot camp leave. He had returned home to Macy and gone with a friend to Walthill (about nine miles from Macy). Eighteen years old and wearing his sailor uniform, he stopped at a store to buy cigarettes. He first saw Joan Neill, 14, and her sister when he left the store. "I asked her if she would write to me if I wrote to her and she said she would. She got pretty well acquainted with the mailman," Martin said, laughing.

The mailman delivered the engagement ring purchased in Honolulu. Martin was discharged on April 15, 1946. He and Joan were married a year later on April 6, 1947. After spending almost three years in the military as a weapons specialist, Martin's best shot has resulted in a 69-year marriage to Joan, the love of his life.

After the war, Martin farmed for four years and then worked at a Hormel Foods meat-packing plant in Fremont, Nebraska, for 35 years, retiring in 1986. For 20 years after retirement, he enjoyed being Santa Claus at the Fremont Mall and delivering Meals on Wheels with Joan.

Lyle and Joan Martin live in Fremont, Nebraska, and have been married for 69 years. Their wedding date is April 6, 1947. They have 3 children, Darryl, Linda, and Rod; 8 grandchildren; and 14 great-grandchildren.

Dale Milligan
Army

◇◇◇◇◇◇◇◇◇◇◇◇◇◇◇◇◇◇◇◇◇◇◇

Birth Date:
Aug. 30, 1924

Hometown:
Fremont, Neb.

Age When Enlisted:
19

Service Dates:
May 1943 –
January 1946

Highest Rank:
Corporal

When Dale Milligan, 92, tells about the buzz bomb fragment removed from his left leg, he simply states he was in the wrong place at the wrong time. The place was close to London and the time was spring 1944.

The German V-1 bomb was nicknamed buzz bomb because of the distinct buzzing sound from the pulse-jet engines powering the bomb. Milligan said he could hear the buzzing noise, something like a small aircraft. Then silence as the bomb plunged toward the ground; upon impact, the 1,870-pound warhead exploded. "I caught a piece of steel in my left leg. By the time they bound me up, they thought my leg was broken so they sent me to the hospital."

He recalled only one or two other patients in that

hospital. After about a week, men injured during fighting on Omaha Beach during the Invasion of Normandy were being admitted. "I said, 'I can't just lie here and do nothing and see these guys coming in.' So, I hobbled around and helped the nurses out. I would wash them [injured soldiers] and clean around where they had been shot. Talk to them." Since that hospital was only for assessment, the injured soon were transferred.

After being hospitalized about two weeks, Milligan returned to his Army company. "I couldn't tell you where we went from one place to the other because I think we moved two or three different places before we got down to the coast to go across the Channel." Crossing the English Channel, the men landed in Normandy on Omaha Beach, which is a region of northern France. This was soon after the Allies had attacked on D-Day, June 6, 1944.

It also was just a little over a year after Milligan was drafted at age 19 on May 19, 1943, and just two days before his Fremont (Nebraska) High School graduation. He wanted to be a turret gunner on a B-17 or B-29 bomber. Instead, he was assigned to the Army 789th AAA (Anti-Aircraft Artillery) Battalion.

After basic training, the entire battalion was sent to Fort Stewart in Georgia. Trained with an artillery unit, Milligan became a marksman with an M1 rifle. He also received training on .30-caliber and .50-caliber machine guns; his position in Europe was machine gunner.

From Georgia, Milligan traveled to Fort Pickett in

Blackstone, Virginia, for advanced training. That training focused on developing proficiency and understanding basic infantry tactics and operations. One infiltration course exercise had the men crawl on their stomachs under barbed wire with machine guns firing above them.

The 789th AAA Battalion of roughly 1,100 men deployed to England in May 1944. The men were issued their .50-caliber machine guns at Croyde Bay where trucks had been shipped with the anti-aircraft guns mounted on trailers, making them portable.

The trailers had their "own little power plant" that enabled a turret, or weapon mount, to rotate 360 degrees. Each turret held four guns. Milligan sat behind a large steel plate that provided some protection from enemy fire. He described the area as "kind of like a cockpit." Looking through a scope similar to binoculars, he focused a red dot on the buzz bombs. "You could fire all four machine guns at one time. There were 660 rounds per minute times four." Those 2,640 rounds came from belt-fed ammunition. Milligan didn't remember how long he could fire at one time. "Usually it was in bursts. I don't even recall how much the case held because it lapped over and back. It was easy once that was fed into your machine gun because it automatically fell down."

Referring to his .50-caliber machine gun training, Milligan said instructors described the following scenario. "What happens if you are out in a place and you don't have any help. You have one of these machine guns and something happens to it. You get hit and you can't see." The men were told to take their machine guns apart and put them back together while blindfolded. "I had to take the back plate off and take the spring out. As I did that, I laid each part down and then put it back together and zeroed in."

After the machine guns were issued at Croyde Bay, Milligan was one of three men selected to provide instruction on the .50-caliber machine gun. "We found out the classes were all for officers. Anyone from a second lieutenant up to a major."

Following completion of those classes, the 789th AAA Battalion had the assignment of providing protection for SHAEF in London. This was the Supreme Headquarters Allied Expeditionary Force under the command of General Dwight D. Eisenhower. American and British troops were both stationed close to SHAEF because Milligan said the Germans "were trying to zero in on General Eisenhower's headquarters." His assignment was to focus on incoming buzz bombs. And that was when Milligan was hit by that buzz bomb fragment.

Following his hospitalization and rejoining his unit, the next movement was to Omaha Beach. Arriving after that battle had ended, Milligan explained that the .50-caliber machine guns were not the type of artillery that could be positioned at the front line on Omaha Beach. "We were not the infantrymen and paratroopers."

Shallow water prevented larger ships from docking close to shore. This was true for the ship on which

Milligan's unit had been transported. LST ships (landing ship, tank) met the larger ship and took men and equipment to shore. The LST was created to support amphibious operations. Production began in 1942 and the first LST ships were operational in October. During the war, a total of 1,051 LST ships were constructed.

Estimating his unit was on Omaha Beach for two to three weeks, Milligan said they waited for the entire battalion to reunite. "We had to sleep in our own tents and sometimes we were getting rain. It was cold." Seeing piles of trash, Milligan started scrounging. "I saw stuff they used when making a runway. I looked at that and told my assistant, 'I think I could make use of that large piece of wire that could be molded and shaped.'" A discarded tarp was placed around the wire.

His assistant asked what Milligan planned to do. "When we get done, we'll know." He proceeded to twist the wire into the shape of a Quonset hut about the height of a refrigerator. Using wood to make bunks and a 25-gallon barrel transformed into a stove, the two men had the makings of living quarters. "We even found some stovepipe and made a door out of some tin." Finding more wood to burn in the stove, Milligan said the quarters were "nice and comfortable."

When the unit was ready to move on, a half dozen men staying behind asked Milligan if the hut could be theirs. He responded: "Whoever claims it first after we move our things out can have it. We can't take it with us."

The men traveled to Belgium in an area around Antwerp where the buzz bombs could be spotted before entering the city. "They started lining all different outfits up and they had 40 millimeter and our .50-calibers. The 90 millimeter could reach clear out, long before the buzz bombs ever got to our position." Those positions changed relative to how the buzz bombs were being directed from Germany toward Antwerp. Allied commanders relied on the port city to handle 40,000 tons of supplies daily. This included docking 1,000 ships, each weighing 19,000 tons. Antwerp had 10 square miles of docks, 20 miles of waterfront and the availability of 600 cranes at the docks to unload supplies.

The battle for Antwerp started late in October 1944 and fighting continued for 154 days. The Germans fired over 5,000 buzz bombs toward Antwerp. The bombs were delivered like a rocket, Milligan said. "I don't think I ever did see the apparatus that they had set up when they shot those off. I don't know how they did that, but Germany had all kinds of ways. They were good at what they succeeded at doing."

From Antwerp, the unit moved toward the Ardennes Mountains where Hitler's troops had launched an attack on the morning of Dec. 16. The Battle of the Bulge continued until Jan. 16, 1945. The unit first set up in the canyon valley close to the only road in the area. After about two days, the unit was moved up the mountain. "One time we were told to grab our barracks bag and jump in the trucks. I said, 'What about our machines?'" The response was simply there was no time; the men had to move and leave the .50-caliber machine guns and 40 mm anti-aircraft weapons. Milligan still argued. "What about the ammunition? It's all loaded and ready to go. All they have to do is jump in the turret and start firing." He admitted: "It's pretty cut and dried. You just jump in the truck and obey orders. We didn't know what we would get back to." Upon return about two days later, everything was as they had left it.

After that victory, the unit was transferred back to its original position "somewhere in Belgium." The unit was preparing to set up along the Rhine River in Germany when the war ended. "We heard a lot of sirens and some of the Germans had moved back into this town. We wondered about all of the noise and inquired about it and they said, 'The war's over!' Then there was more noise."

Probably also making some noise was Milligan's brother, Ralph, who served in India. Two other brothers, Luther and Clifford, worked at the Mead (Nebraska) Ordnance Plant.

At the end of the war, the 789th AAA Battalion broke up and the men were sent to different locations. "Some of us guarded an airfield outside Stuttgart, Germany." Milligan thought it was December 1945 when he finally boarded a ship in Le Havre, France, for the U.S. Passing the Statue of Liberty and then disembarking in New York City, Milligan remembered seeing lots of people. Perhaps feeling he was in the wrong place at the wrong time, he said, "They put us on the train and I said I don't think this is any town where I would want to come back."

And he never did.

◇◇◇◇◇◇◇◇◇◇◇◇◇◇◇◇◇◇◇◇◇◇◇◇

After the war, Milligan served as a military escort for a year. For eligibility he had to re-enlist, and he accompanied the deceased on trains to final destinations. As a corporal, Milligan could accompany only those who were his rank or below. As a civilian, he worked primarily in sales and retired in 1987. Milligan lived in Colorado for 30 years and moved back to Fremont, Nebraska, in 2009.

Dale Milligan lives in Fremont, Nebraska, and was married to Josephine for 51 years. Their wedding date is Oct. 19, 1957. They have 3 children, Larry, Glenda Rae, and Barbara; 4 grandchildren; and 2 step-great-grandchildren.

Raymond Mitchell
Army Air Corps

◇◇◇◇◇◇◇◇◇◇◇◇◇◇◇◇◇◇◇

Birth Date:
Oct. 21, 1922

Hometown:
Grandview, Wash.

Age When Enlisted:
20

Service Dates:
October 1942 –
October 1945

Highest Rank:
Staff Sergeant

One more mission. For Ray Mitchell, 94, it would be his 24th mission on a B-17 bomber. After 25 missions, he could go home to Grandview, Washington. "But we didn't make it back, so that one didn't count. It was 23."

Mitchell enlisted in the Army Air Corps after he turned 20 on Oct. 21, 1942. He wanted to be a fighter pilot but didn't have the required two years of college. He completed basic training at Keesler Field (Biloxi, Mississippi).

Before traveling to Mississippi, Mitchell explained that in Washington he had worked with the Civilian Conservation Corps (CCC). One of the first New Deal programs, the CCC promoted environmental conservation. Nearly 3 million young men were involved with the CCC. They lived in camps operated by the Army. The military-like discipline they received proved beneficial when large numbers of men either enlisted or were drafted during World War II.

Because of his experience in the CCC before entering the service, Mitchell said: "I was tougher than the 18-year-old kid. I did construction work for the government and was paid $30 a month. I got $8 of it and sent the rest of it back home for my family."

After basic training, Mitchell attended Armament School at Lowry Air Force Base (Denver, Colorado); specialized training on the B-17 at Gunnery School (Wendover, Utah); first phase heavy bomber training at Moses Lake Army Air Base (Moses Lake, Washington); and 2nd and 3rd phase training at Kearney Army Air Force Base (Kearney, Nebraska). The Kearney base became a training field for combat crews.

In May 1943, Mitchell and the 100th Bombardment Group arrived in England. Mitchell's 10-man crew in the 100th Bombardment Group of the Eighth Air Force left base in eastern England on May 28, 1944. Heavy machine guns were mounted at the front, back, top, bottom and sides of a four-engine B-17, nicknamed the Flying Fortress. Each bombing mission included Mitchell's squadron of 21 B-17s. Destination on May 28 was an oil refinery in Magdeburg, Germany (just under 100 miles from Berlin). The B-17 was carrying 12 bombs, each weighing 500 pounds. "As we crossed the English Channel, we encountered very heavy flak [anti-aircraft fire]. Our altitude was 30,000 feet and the temperature [inside the B-17] was 60 degrees below zero."

Open to the outside air, the planes were unheated. The crew wore heavy gloves and electrically heated suits. Oxygen masks were available. "As we approached the target, about 20 ME 109s [Germany's principle fighter planes] attacked us. We suffered heavy damage and the airplane was on fire."

It was 10 minutes after 2. The crew was ordered to bail out. As a waist gunner, Mitchell provided protection of the aircraft from enemy attacks directed at the mid-section of the plane. His position was behind the bomb bay about the middle of the plane. Because he was close to the escape hatch, Mitchell thought he would be first to bail out. "When you go off oxygen you have to hustle out." He explained how pulling a cable attached to the escape hatch released it. "You have super strength at a time like this. I pulled apparently at too much of an angle and broke it. This is almost an impossible situation now because you can't bail out if the escape hatch isn't gone."

Finally able to get the escape hatch to release, Mitchell was ready to jump when the B-17 went into a spin. "It slammed me down on the floor. My radio operator landed on my back." Estimating the aircraft was at an altitude of about 15,000 feet, Mitchell was beginning to see trees and fenceposts and Germans. "Every time we made a revolution, I could see the sky and then the ground then the sky then the ground and it isn't very far away. You think about everything you did when a little kid. It's not going to hurt me; it's going to hurt the people back home."

Then the plane broke in half. Mitchell and the radio operator were pulled outside. Mitchell managed to attach his chest-type parachute. The parachutes were too bulky to wear inside the B-17, but each crew member wore a harness, allowing him to quickly clip on the parachute. He pulled the rip cord. "It was a relief to see 28 feet of silk up there. It was just 700 feet — not 7,000 — before I hit the ground." Upon landing in a field, he sprained his right ankle. "It wasn't long until the Germans showed up." Of the original 21 B-17s in the squadron, only one aircraft was shot down on May 28. "That was us."

The marching began. Officers were separated from the other men. Even with a sprained ankle, Mitchell walked. "Had to walk seven miles to a town and were taken to an airbase." That's where he heard three of his crew members had died when the B-17 was shot down. Along with Mitchell, the pilot and five other crew members had been captured.

Over the next weeks, Mitchell and the other prisoners of war (POWs) were in different cities and temporary POW camps. In Frankfurt, he was intensely interrogated. "You're not supposed to weaken and talk, so it was a lot of Staff Sergeant Raymond J. Mitchell, 39460300, U.S.A." The eight-digit number was his serial number. "You say that over and over and over. They ask you what group you're from, what kind of airplane you were flying, what altitude were you when you came across the Channel, things like that. Then you just repeat your name, rank and serial number."

At one point, the men were put in train boxcars for eight days and eight nights. "They didn't move the train. Just sat in the boxcars." The last 14 days of marching ended at Stalag VII A, located just north of Moosburg in southern Bavaria. It was the largest German POW camp and covered an area of 86 acres.

Because he was a non-commissioned officer, "They didn't make us work." Men played cards, baseball and softball. Diversions. There also was lots of walking. "There was a warning rail around the inside of the compound and we were allowed to walk there. From the warning rail there was a no man's land and then about 20 feet of barbed wire entanglement and a fence about 15 feet high." The Germans made it clear to the prisoners that there would be no escape from the camp. "It was absolutely impossible to escape from."

Two weeks after Mitchell's B-17 was shot down, his father, Robert, was sent the first of two Western Union telegrams. It was dated June 11, 1944. "The Secretary of War desires me to express his deep regret that your son Staff Sergeant Raymond J Mitchell has been reported missing in action since twenty eight May over Germany. If further details or other information are received you will be promptly notified." It was signed Ulio The Adjutant General. James Alexander Ulio served as Adjutant General of the U.S. Army from 1942-46.

Twenty-seven days later, the second telegram was addressed to Mitchell's father. Dated July 8, 1944, it said: "Report just received through the International Red Cross states that your son Staff Sergeant Raymond J Mitchell is a prison of war of the German government letter of information follows from Provost Marshall General." Major General Allen W. Gullion was the Provost Marshall General. His staff position was to handle investigations and incarcerations of U.S. Army personnel.

Meals at the prisoner of war camp often consisted of moldy bread and some kind of thin soup. "The food was terrible. We ate twice a day. A cup of lousy tea in the morning and slice of moldy bread. In the evening, we had plain, boiled potatoes or a type of mush." Knowing that was the extent of his food, Mitchell replied: "I didn't give a damn what it tasted like. I was going to eat it." When captured, he weighed 185 pounds; when liberated, he weighed 135 pounds.

Infrequently, the prisoners received a Red Cross package that included chocolate, cigarettes and soap. Mitchell described personal hygiene at Moosburg as terrible. To pass time, the men sat and smoked and filled a coffee can with cigarette butts.

Was he ever ill? "How about mentally ill? That's tough. We knew the United States was going to win, but how many years was it going to take? Going to stay here and stay here and stay here." While a POW, Mitchell thought about freedom. "That goes through your mind all the time. It was never any doubt in our minds who was going to win the war, but whether you were going to be around when it was over. This is a thing that isn't in the back of your mind, it's foremost all the time. I know that I say that for, I believe, everybody who was there."

The prisoners were able to hear how the war was progressing. "Having a lot of radio operators, it wasn't too hard to put a radio together with the right pieces. It wasn't too long before we had a radio. That was our line to the outside world." They listened to BBC (British Broadcasting Corporation) broadcasts. "Some guy would copy down the news and then he'd go from one place to the other and read it. They [Germans] knew we had a radio but could never find it. It would always disappear. Seems like after every broadcast they'd come looking for it. Things were not too enjoyable at those times. I was never beaten, never hit with a rifle butt, but that doesn't mean they [German guards] didn't do it, because they did."

Mitchell was always with other men. "You would go nuts if by yourself." Every day was just another day. His 22nd birthday was Oct. 21, 1944. Just another day. Christmas. That was very difficult for some men. Mitchell asked for anything from any prisoner's lunch. He combined those contributions in a helmet to create a makeshift cake so some prisoners could have a Christmas treat.

January, February, March and April — every day, except one, during those first four months of 1945 was just like the previous seven months. The exception was

April 29. Around 9 a.m., gunfire was heard. "As the day progressed, the guards knew they were going to be the prisoners and we were going to be the people who were free. We gave them our utensils and our little skillets we had made out of tin cans, little pots they could boil water in."

It was 10 minutes after 12 in the afternoon when an American flag was raised. Men from the Third Army threw toothbrushes, toothpaste, candy and cigarettes over the fence. Referring to some of the Third Army men, Mitchell stated: "They said, 'This is crazy! You guys are free!'" It wasn't long before Sherman tanks crashed through the fence that surrounded the POW camp. "Literally, thousands of prisoners bolted out of there."

On May 1, General George S. Patton Jr., commander of the Third Army, arrived at Moosburg "in his jeep with his dog, and a pistol on each hip." It was two days after liberation and Mitchell was still in the camp. "I was a POW about 11 months and a few days, but before I finally got out, another 10 days had elapsed because I was one of the last to leave."

Before leaving, men took showers and were given clean clothes. "The main event was delousing. The bugs were eating us up. Couldn't do a thing about it either. Would be scratching and itching. We wore the same clothes month after month."

Mitchell was on the USS *Lejeune* for 14 days during his return to the U.S. "It was like coming home on a rowboat." Heading into New York Harbor, he saw her — the Statue of Liberty. "That impresses you. A lot of them [former prisoners] were crying." Mitchell said he didn't cry during his time as a prisoner of war, nor when he saw the Statue of Liberty. However, after a long train ride to Grandview, Washington, he finally cried. His mother had died but his father was there. "I could cry. I was home." Also home were older brother, Floyd, who served in the Navy, and younger brother, Lee, who was in the Army Air Corps.

After a 60-day leave at home, Mitchell traveled to California for three weeks of convalescent leave. Then in October 1945, he was discharged in Denver, Colorado. In Denver he also reconnected with a woman he had met when he was at Lowry Air Force Base where bomber aircrews were trained. There were many dances at the Rainbow Ballroom in Denver. "They had to entertain us."

Once Mitchell saw Delma Ernst standing against the wall and asked her to dance. He got her address and they corresponded during his time in the service, although mail was limited when Mitchell was a POW. "I don't remember about how many letters we could write, but it wasn't too many. We were allowed to have a couple of packages. My family sent packages; I never got them until just a few days before we left."

It was Dec. 8, 1945, when Ray and Delma married. It was 56 years after he was a prisoner of war when the Mitchells returned to England and Germany in June 2000. They saw the airstrip from where his B-17 bomber took off on May 28, 1944. In Germany, through an interpreter, they talked with a man who as a young boy had kept a journal throughout the war. He took the Mitchells to where the B-17 bomber was shot down.

Almost 72 years after his service in the Army Air Corps, including just over 11 months as a prisoner of war, Staff Sergeant Raymond J. Mitchell, 39460300, U.S.A., asked a question and quickly answered it. "Was I proud to serve? You bet."

◇◇◇◇◇◇◇◇◇◇◇◇◇◇◇◇◇◇◇◇

After the war, Mitchell worked at a Hormel Foods meat-packing plant in Fremont, Nebraska, for 30 years. He retired in 1977 as a foreman.

Ray Mitchell lives in Fremont, Nebraska, and was married to Delma for 64 years. Their wedding date is Dec. 8, 1945. They have 3 children, Marcia, Donna, and Monte; 4 grandchildren; and 2 great-grandchildren.

Kenneth Mussman
Army

◇◇◇◇◇◇◇◇◇◇◇◇◇◇◇◇◇◇◇◇◇◇◇◇◇

Birth Date:
March 22, 1921

Hometown:
Alexandria, Neb.

Age When Drafted:
21

Service Dates:
October 1942 –
January 1946

Highest Rank:
Technician,
Fifth Grade

Kenny Mussman, 95, admitted if he hadn't been drafted into the Army, he probably wouldn't have enlisted. However, he was quick to add that it was his duty and he is proud of his service.

A 1939 graduate of Alexandria High School, Mussman said times were hard and there were no jobs in Nebraska. He was helping his father on the family farm and had the opportunity to work in Idaho in September 1939. "I was gone four weeks and I picked potatoes. I came home with $80 and spent it all on a 1931 Model A that had 40,000 miles on it."

Back in Nebraska on Dec. 7, 1941, Mussman clearly remembered that day. "It was a Sunday and we were driving home from church. We heard on the radio that

Pearl Harbor had been struck." He was 20 years old.

The Selective Training and Service Act of 1940 required all men between the ages of 21 and 45 to register for the draft. After he turned 21 on March 22, 1942, he drove to the nearest high school in the county to register. He received an Order to Report for Induction letter dated June 30, 1942.

The letter informed Mussman ". . . you are hereby notified that you have now been selected for training and service in the Army." He reported to the local board in Fairbury on Oct. 20, 1942, where he caught a train destined for Fort Leavenworth, Kansas. Upon arrival around 11 p.m., about 50 men were assigned to their barracks. "They were trying to teach us to make our bed." It was a long process. "The sergeant would come around after you had made the bed and he would rip the corner off and say, 'Make it over again.'" So, the beds were made over again and over again.

Finally around midnight the men got to bed, but four hours later someone tapped Mussman on his shoulder. "Soldier, you're on KP." In the kitchen, another soldier was already sitting and Mussman was told to sit in a second chair. "In between the two chairs was 100 pounds of potatoes for us to peel. We peeled until 11 o'clock that morning." Making and remaking beds and peeling pounds and pounds of potatoes created a lasting image. "I can see today why they wanted to impress they were in charge."

A more difficult reminder occurred after Mussman left Fort Leavenworth the first part of December for basic training in Fort Warren, Wyoming. "I got a phone call from the Red Cross that my grandfather had died. Fort Warren and where my grandfather died in Fillmore County [Nebraska] is not very far apart." He asked for a three-day pass to attend the funeral, but the request was denied. "At that time, it seemed terrible, but after a while it kind of sunk in that they were in charge."

Basic training in Wyoming during December meant some days with temperatures below zero. "We had a lot of guys from the South who were getting sick because they weren't used to this extreme cold weather." Because of the increased number of troops, more than 280 wooden buildings had been constructed for temporary housing. Without insulation and interior walls, the buildings were cold during Wyoming winters.

About a month and a half after his arrival at Fort Warren, Mussman returned to Nebraska and reported to Fort Crook near Omaha. At Fort Crook, he took classes at the Ordnance Technical Training School. Instruction included both theory and practical training in the disassembling, adjustment, replacement of parts, repair and reassembling of Army automotive vehicles. He worked on cars, jeeps and 6-wheel drive trucks. A farm boy, Mussman said, "I think they picked farm boys because they probably knew a lot of them had mechanical experience having been around tractors."

Mussman had one more relocation in the U.S. before he was sent overseas. He continued working in mechanics for about a year at Camp Atterbury in Indiana. In February 1942, construction started at Camp Atterbury that is located 46 miles northeast of Bloomington. Seven months later, 1,780 buildings had been constructed. Over 275,000 soldiers received training at Camp Atterbury during World War II. The base also served as an internment camp for approximately 15,000 Italian and German prisoners of war.

On April 1, 1944, Mussman's unit left for North Africa. His first night after arrival brought a reminder that a war was being fought. "Our unit was small and we went to a soccer stadium. Instead of pitching tents, we laid on the benches in the stadium. Maybe about 2 or 3 o'clock the air raid siren went off." The commanding officer led his men into a wine cellar where African natives also were huddled for protection. No bombing occurred, but everyone still had to take cover.

It was hot and miserable in Africa, but Mussman only had to stay for a couple of months. Seventeen volunteers were needed and told they would "go to an island where the prettiest girls in the world are." Fifteen men already had volunteered when Mussman became number 17. Sergeant Lloyd from Wisconsin raised his own hand and then grabbed Mussman's arm and thrust it into the air. "You've got 17," the Wisconsinite said. Soon the 17 volunteers were on a plane to Corsica, the island with "the prettiest girls in the world." Located in the Mediterranean Sea and belonging to France, Corsica is about 100 miles southeast of Nice, France, and 50 miles west of Tuscany, Italy. Packed in the plane like sardines, "We landed in a field and bounced three or four times." But, they weren't on Corsica; they were on Sardinia, which is Italy's second largest island. The two islands are about 133 air miles apart.

Once the pilot got reoriented and landed in Corsica, Mussman thought six to eight trucks were loaded on an LST ship (landing ship, tank). Production of the LST began in October 1942. They were built so the ship could approach closely to beaches to unload cargo. Mussman explained that after the ship got as close as it could to a beach, a large door at the front end was opened downward and the trucks were driven right from the water to the land.

After the trucks were loaded and chained in position, the LST with Mussman and the other 16 volunteers headed for southern France. "We had some stormy weather while on the sea and one of the trucks broke loose, and with that truck loose, it hit the next truck and then that broke loose. We had quite a mess until the storm was over." Before the Mediterranean Sea began getting rough, Mussman had been sleeping under a truck. When the weather got worse, he crawled out and tried to sleep inside a truck cab. That's when the first truck broke loose and began hitting another truck. Inside a cab became the safest place to be. No one was hurt, but Mussman admitted everyone was relieved when the storm subsided. It took approximately 10½ hours for the ship to arrive in Marseille, France.

Mussman remained in France from the first part of July 1944 until the end of December 1945. After Germany surrendered on May 7, 1945, he was given orders to paint certain letters on truck bumpers. "I asked the lieutenant what the letters stood for. One was R and he said, 'Rangoon and that's where you are going.'" Mussman had no idea the location of Rangoon but guessed the South Pacific. Rangoon was the capital city of Burma and located in southeastern Asia.

Because the Japanese surrendered on Sept. 2, Mussman never had to ship off to Rangoon. Instead, his unit was sent home in December 1945. "I think there were 6,000 of us on a ship and five deep in a canvas bed." On Jan. 1, 1946, he walked to the deck early because when the ship passed the Statue of Liberty he wanted to see it. After the ship docked in New Jersey, he just wanted to get his feet back on solid ground.

He also wanted to see a girlfriend at home. Two years earlier in December 1944 while in North Africa, Mussman sent money to his brother. "I told him to go buy a diamond ring and give it to Nadine [Weber]." So, Nadine and Leonard went out for a cup of coffee. "My brother proposed for me," Mussman said, laughing. Nadine said yes and Jan. 12, 1946, was the first time he saw Nadine wearing the engagement ring. "I thought she looked pretty nice and so did the ring."

Typed on his Separation Qualification Record dated Jan. 9, 1946, is a Summary of Military Occupations. It reads: "Stationed with the 393rd Ordnance Medium Automotive Maintenance Company in Africa, Corsica and France, served as mechanic in adjusting, replacing worn or broken parts, repairing and overhauling army wheel and track vehicles. Did this work in fixed shops and in the field over all types of terrain, in all types of weather and under severe combat conditions."

Also listed on the separation qualification record are civilian occupations. As a general farmhand the following description is given: "Helped father, W.C. Mussman, operated 320 acre general farm in Jefferson County, Nebraska, for approximately 8 years ending in October, 1942. Drove teams and tractors in plowing, seeding, cultivating and harvesting corn, small grains and hay. Helped feed and care for beef and dairy cattle, hogs and poultry. Made necessary maintenance repairs to farm buildings, implements, trucks and tractors. Drove 1½-ton truck in hauling farm products, livestock and grain to market."

Referring to those military and civilian occupations, Mussman said he has a memorable date from his military years and a memorable date from his civilian years. "I went into the service on Oct. 20, 1942, and I got married on Oct. 20, 1946."

Before he left for his military service, his father gave Mussman three calves. Upon his return, those three calves were cows and had their own calves. When they moved to their own farm, Kenny and Nadine had eight or nine head of cattle to begin their married life. And, Kenny had gained experience in the Army to help maintain the farm equipment.

◇◇◇◇◇◇◇◇◇◇◇◇◇◇◇◇◇◇◇◇◇

After the war, Mussman farmed near Ohiowa, Nebraska, for 14 years. He served as Ohiowa postmaster for 15 years and then was a rural mail carrier for 22 years. Mussman was a rural mail carrier in Geneva, Nebraska, when he retired in 1997.

Kenny and Nadine Mussman live in Fremont, Nebraska, and have been married for 70 years. Their wedding date is Oct. 20, 1946. They have 5 children, Kathren, Johnell, Gaylord, Burnell, and David; 14 grandchildren; and 12 great-grandchildren.

James Peterson
Army

◇◇◇◇◇◇◇◇◇◇◇◇◇◇◇◇◇◇◇◇◇◇

Birth Date:
March 9, 1923

Hometown:
Fremont, Neb.

Age When Enlisted:
20

Service Dates:
February 1943 –
January 1946

Highest Rank:
Private First Class

Is there such a thing as too much marching in the Army? Just ask Jim Peterson, 93, who, after marching drills during basic training in 1943, continued marching. He was a member of the 86th Infantry Division band. As a Fremont (Nebraska) High School student, Peterson learned to play the oboe. When he enlisted in the Army at age 20, he was aware of the Army band.

Before he and about 20 friends took a bus from Fremont to Fort Crook outside of Omaha, Nebraska, Peterson had wanted to enlist in the Navy. "But I was color-blind so they wouldn't accept me. That did keep me from driving an Army vehicle, but I could play oboe and be in the band."

The 86th Infantry Division (nickname, Blackhawk

Division) had basic training at Camp Howze, near Gaines-ville, Texas. When Peterson arrived, the division band was already partially formed. The band was under the direction of a warrant officer and Peterson reported that he played oboe. "That's all it took. There were very few oboe players." In addition to oboe, he also could play drums and alto horn.

During his 8- to 10-week stay at Camp Howze, the band played in retreat parades and for bond drives. Peterson explained a general observed the band and troops during retreat parades that were held strictly on base. To promote the purchase of war bonds, the 86th Infantry Division Band played at the Cotton Bowl stadium in Dallas and other sites across the country. During the war, the United States Treasury offered Americans an opportunity to invest in their country and their futures. A $25 war bond could be purchased for $18.75. Ten years from the time of purchase, the bond could be redeemed for $25.

According to the United States History website (www. u-s-history.com), more than 85 million Americans (half the population) purchased bonds that totaled $185.7 billion. "Those incredible results, due to the mass selling efforts of helping to finance the war, have never since been matched."

Peterson returned to Nebraska during his first furlough of about 10 days and married Dorothy Heggstedt in June 1943. They met when both were working at the Fairmont Creamery in Fremont and had been dating for about a year before Peterson enlisted. "I was still 20; my mother had to sign for me to get married." His father had died when Peterson was 12.

During his assignments throughout the United States, Dorothy accompanied her husband. Their first location was Camp Livingston in northern Louisiana from November 1943 until September 1944. "We took the train, lived off base and Dorothy got a government job." For their first Christmas away from Nebraska, it was assumed the Petersons would experience warmer temperatures in the South. "It was nasty weather. Very seldom did things freeze down there." Ironically, he said, it rained and then froze on the trees. "Some of the tents had holes in them from the ice falling off the trees and into the tents."

Time in Louisiana meant daily maneuvers. The band also continued to practice and participate in retreat parades. After about 10 months in Louisiana, Peterson received clearance to drive an officer's wife and Dorothy to Napa, California. The Packard convertible he drove belonged to the captain's wife. Peterson reported to Camp San Luis Obispo, about 200 miles northwest of Los Angeles.

Men in the division participated in amphibious training for about a week in La Jolla, about 310 miles south of Camp San Luis Obispo. The men jumped off landing crafts and waded to shore carrying their rifles and field packs. Then they climbed a rope ladder to the top of a cliff. This training simulated landings the men could encounter when they arrived at the Pacific islands.

"We were slated to go to the Pacific and then there was fighting at the Battle of the Bulge [Dec. 16, 1944, to Jan. 25,

1945]. They needed more infantry there, so we hopped on a troop train and left California for Boston." It was Feb. 9, 1945, and Peterson said the train traveling to the East Coast followed various alternating routes — even going into Canada — for fear of sabotage. Even though the Battle of the Bulge was over, "There still was combat and things were pretty shaky at the time."

With an overseas destination, Peterson explained the band no longer had practices. Members still took their instruments and played at a couple of officers' funerals.

The men left Boston on March 2 for combat in Germany. They traveled on the Swedish liner *Kungsholm* that had been converted to a troop transport. "We were lead ship in the convoy of three or four other ships in a rough Atlantic Ocean." The ship dropped depth charges and followed a zigzag pattern because of the presence of German submarines. "There were many sick GIs."

The *Kungsholm* docked in Le Havre Harbor in northwestern France and the men went to Camp Old Gold. This camp was one of several located across the country that was named after American cigarette brands. Others included: Camp Lucky Strike, Camp Chesterfield, Camp Pall Mall and Camp Philip Morris.

Heading for positions along the west bank of the Rhine River (near Cologne, Germany), the infantrymen were transported on 40/8 railroad boxcars. Originally designed for 40 men or 8 horses, the boxcars were first used during World War I. Peterson estimated each car held about 40 men who sat on straw that was strewn across the floor. The distance from Le Havre to Cologne was about 369 miles.

The Rhine River serves as a border between Germany and France and men of the 86th Infantry Division were positioned along its banks from March 27 to April 4, 1945. "At first, it was kind of nasty. But after that, the Germans kind of started to collapse and some of them were giving up and walking in on our lines."

When German soldiers were captured, Peterson drove a truck and took the prisoners from the front line back to division headquarters. "Day after day for a while we were picking up prisoners." Peterson clarified even though he was not allowed to drive an Army vehicle while in the U.S. because he was color-blind, he could drive when overseas.

During one night transport, Peterson was driving "with just two little tiny lights." Shots were fired at the truck. He floored the gas pedal, ducked down as far as he could and drove as fast as the truck would go. The next morning he noticed the truck had been hit. "There was a bullet hole on the passenger side and it had gone just over the gas pedal and just missed my foot."

Usually only one guard accompanied Peterson when prisoners were in the truck. The guard rode in the back of the truck with the prisoners who were frisked; their hands were not tied. Peterson described the POWs as very quiet and docile. "They'd been on the road for years. Not much equipment left, any clothes or anything else."

However, one possible prisoner was not quiet and did get away. Peterson was on guard duty one night. He heard artillery fire and then heard another noise. "Who's there?" No answer. "Come to find out it was a big raccoon walking around and dragging branches." Peterson laughed and added, "I was ready to shoot."

From the Rhine to the Ruhr region of western Germany, Peterson said his division "cleaned up the rear pocket." The men were looking for snipers "who felt they still wanted to fight. There was activity but not to the extent there had been." Band members served as MPs (military police) while the division moved through areas that had seen combat. "We led the convoys if we were moving the troops. I was on the autobahn, which was bombed out, but we had picked up German motorcycles and were riding them so we could get around."

As men of the 86th Infantry Division kept moving through Germany, they stayed in vacant houses at night. "We even went through some castles."

While moving into Bavaria and finally Austria, word was received that Germany had surrendered on May 7, 1945. "We were at a beautiful mountain lake home in the Swiss Alps on V-E Day [Victory in Europe, May 8]." The home belonged to people who had fled Vienna. The men were served Viennese wine and cookies. "To tell you the truth, I don't remember the rest of the afternoon."

After approximately three months in Europe, Peterson returned to the U.S. "We were the first infantry outfit redeployed through the States to the Pacific." He had a 30-day furlough and was on a troop train in Phoenix, Arizona, ready for transport to the Pacific, when word was received that Japan had surrendered on Aug. 15. "On V-J [Victory over Japan, Sept. 2] afternoon, we kept on going to San Francisco."

He took a Liberty ship (class of cargo ship) to Luzon, Philippines. "I had more ship time than some of the sailors did." The ship stopped at a refueling station in the Pacific for about a week because Peterson said he believed, "They didn't know where to put us."

At Luzon, the men built a base camp where they stayed about six weeks and then moved up to Manila. Time was spent looking for snipers hiding in the jungle, but Peterson never went into the jungle. Men in the 86th Infantry Division Band "stayed close to the Red Cross tent and USO girls." The United Service Organizations, Inc. was founded on Feb. 4, 1941, when Franklin D. Roosevelt was president. During the war, nearly 1.5 million Americans volunteered their services in some way to provide live entertainment for troops.

Peterson left the Philippines and was discharged on Jan. 30, 1946. He went home to Dorothy and a baby daughter in Omaha. Karen was born on Oct. 15, 1945, while he was in the Philippines. "I didn't know it for a week."

Any regrets during his three years of service? Two. Peterson had to be away from Dorothy for extended periods of time and he didn't see his daughter until she was

4 months old. However, he definitely has never missed all that marching he did in the Army.

◇◇◇◇◇◇◇◇◇◇◇◇◇◇◇◇◇◇◇◇

After the war, Peterson was employed as a bookkeeper for Texaco stations in Nebraska (Fremont and Blair). During that time, he took classes at Midland Lutheran College (Fremont, Nebraska) and graduated with an accounting degree. In 1951, Peterson began working for the Fremont Department of Utilities. He retired in 1985.

Jim and Phyllis Peterson live in Fremont, Nebraska, and have been married for 20 years. Their wedding date is Dec. 23, 1995. Jim also was married to Dorothy for 10 years. They have 4 children, Karen, Carol, Mark, and Bryan; 4 grandchildren; and 5 great-grandchildren. Phyllis has 2 sons, Randy and Greg; 2 grandchildren; and 1 great-grandchild.

Melvin Schwanke
Marine Corps

◇◇◇◇◇◇◇◇◇◇◇◇◇◇◇◇◇◇◇◇◇

Birth Date:
March 14, 1926

Hometown:
Fremont, Neb.

Age When Enlisted:
17

Service Dates:
June 1944 –
May 1946

Highest Rank:
Corporal

A father who was an Army officer in World War I would be proud to have his son enlist in the Army during World War II. But what happened when the son wanted to enlist in the Marine Corps? Mel Schwanke, 90, said his father hollered in resistance. And since a 17-year-old enlistee would need parental permission, the paper would not be signed. "So, I talked my mom into signing my papers." It was a life-changing experience.

Schwanke was a senior at Fremont (Nebraska) High School when Marine Corps recruiters visited the school. He decided to enlist and then had to confront his parents. "They [recruiters] did their job very well." He was allowed to graduate before reporting for active duty.

On June 19, 1944, Schwanke joined the Marines and soon boarded a train with Johnnie Stout, another Fremont High School graduate, for boot camp in California.

A year after he became a Marine, Schwanke would be faced with his most life-changing experience of the war.

First, he had eight weeks at boot camp and Schwanke said discipline was very strict. "You learn to be a number." One training exercise had the Marines crawling on their stomachs under barbed wire while real bullets were being shot above their heads.

"We were told real bullets were being used where we were going, so we had to learn to dodge real bullets. You have to learn your lessons well as it will save your life someday." There were injuries — and deaths — when men didn't pay attention and didn't stay low to the ground.

Schwanke referred to real bullets when, at the completion of boot camp, he was standing next to Stout. "We counted off one, two, one, two. I was a one and Johnny was a two. Johnny went to Iwo Jima and was killed there."

When Schwanke left Nebraska for California, it was his first time away from home. "I didn't let it bother me." However, while in the Marine Corps, Schwanke admitted, "It was pretty special to receive mail." His mother and sister, Velda, wrote letters.

As an infantry rifleman, Schwanke was trained on firing the Browning Automatic Rifle (BAR). The .30-caliber rifle was an air-cooled, gas-operated, magazine-fed weapon. Equipped with a bipod, the BAR weighed 20 pounds and could fire 120-150 rounds per minute. "That bothered me because my religious background was not to kill."

After eight more weeks of advanced training, Schwanke and 62 additional men of Company E, 2nd Battalion, 1st Marines were ready to ship out to the South Pacific. Their destination was the island of Peleliu, which is present-day Palau. Operation Stalemate II was the codename for the Battle of Peleliu, fought from Sept. 15 to Nov. 27, 1944. The volcanic island is about 6 miles long and about 2 miles wide.

On Peleliu, the Marines got a foretaste of what would confront them on Okinawa. More than 10,000 Japanese troops were securing the island. Interconnected tunnels in caves provided the Japanese hiding places from Allied forces and their weapons.

One objective of the 1st Marine Division (17,490 men) and the Army 81st Infantry Division (10,944 men) was to capture Peleliu's airfield. The 1st Marines arrived on the island about a week before control of the island was taken from the Japanese. The division was in combat for 10 days.

The number of U.S. casualties and wounded was heavy during the Battle of Peleliu, resulting in a higher death toll than any other amphibious assault in U.S. military history. Approximately 28,000 Marines and infantry troops were engaged in fighting; 40 percent either died or were wounded. Schwanke said no one in his battalion was killed or sustained injuries.

When the battalion left Peleliu, it went to Pavuvu (the largest of the Russell Islands) for what Schwanke called rest camp. Remaining there for a couple of weeks, the men continued with .30-caliber rifle practice and other on-ground training.

Leaving Pavuvu, the next stop for the Marines was the island of Okinawa, a travel distance of 3,225 miles. "We sailed on a very crowded troop ship. It was hot and smelly because many were seasick by the time we got near Okinawa." The ship was outfitted with lots of bunk beds. "You wanted to be higher up because of all the seasickness."

On Easter Sunday, April 1, 1945, the naval ship arrived at Okinawa, which is Japan's fifth largest island. For almost three months (April 1 to June 22) the Battle of Okinawa would be the first and only U.S. land operation on Japanese soil.

Nicknamed Operation Iceberg, it was the largest amphibious assault, the last major battle in the Pacific Theater and the bloodiest campaign in the Pacific. There were more than 250,000 total casualties. Together with the 1st Marine Division, the 6th Marine Division and five divisions of the 10th Army, a total of 183,000 troops fought on Okinawa. It was the largest number under one commander (Army Lieutenant-General Simon B. Buckner, Jr.) ever assembled during the war in the Pacific.

When about 60,000 troops landed on the west coast of Okinawa on April 1, 1945, the naval ship was too large to dock close to the beach, so the men boarded smaller amphibious landing crafts called LSTs (landing ship, tank). Because the LST also could not get close enough to the beach, a ramp was lowered at the front. Schwanke said the men had "to march right into the deep water, sink to the bottom and then walk in and march up the beach."

Each Marine wore a field transport pack weighing 65 pounds. Items inside the pack included food rations, first aid pouch and entrenching tool, a shovel used to dig a foxhole or trench. Each Marine had a canteen attached to his belt. His Browning Automatic Rifle weighed 20 pounds. Carrying this load, Schwanke said men drowned because they couldn't swim to shore. Anyone who made it to the beach had to quickly clean his weapon because the Japanese were firing at the Marines.

Okinawa is about 60 miles long and ranges between 2 and 18 miles wide. Overtaking Okinawa would be a major Allied victory because it is located just 350 miles from Kyushu (the southernmost of Japan's major islands). If the four airfields on the island were under American control, planes could reach all of Japan's industrial centers without having to refuel during a round trip.

Terrain and weather were not pleasant, Schwanke said. Two-thirds of the island is mountainous and forested. Excessive rain meant slow movement through mud. High temperatures, together with the rain, resulted in high humidity.

Also, the Japanese were occupying numerous caves. They had constructed an estimated 60 miles of interconnected passages in tunnels and that made combat on Okinawa difficult, Schwanke said.

A hastily dug one-man foxhole served as protection from enemy fire and as a place to sleep. "The hardest time was at night. The Japanese would holler, 'Corpsman. Corpsman' [medic]. So, you would think it was a wounded buddy lying out there. But it was a way to get us to expose our position. Had to keep quiet and try to sleep."

Another difficulty was food. The Marines carried individual food rations. "We had canned milk, canned cheese and Spam. When we ran out, we caught chickens, pigs and other wild animals." If the men came across an empty cave, sometimes the Japanese had left food.

Seven days before the Americans secured Okinawa, Schwanke had his most life-changing experience of the war on June 12, 1945. Of his original platoon of 63, he was one of only five men who had not been killed on the island.

"We had some Japanese trapped in a cave under us and we were lobbing hand grenades down at them and they were throwing hand grenades up at us. Sometimes we would catch them and throw them back down and they would explode immediately."

Because he was on a walkie-talkie to call for a flame-thrower tank as reinforcement to help get control of the cave, Schwanke was distracted. Suddenly, a buddy yelled, "Mel, get rid of that thing at your feet." It was a Japanese hand grenade.

"I went to reach for the sucker and it went off right in my face." He explained the grenades were made of scrap metal, so metal pieces shot in all directions when they exploded.

"One piece severed my watch band, one went in right next to my eye and my hearing was affected. Lots of pieces lodged in my stomach, in my leg and arms and a big one by my spine."

A buddy carried Schwanke, unconscious and bleeding profusely, to a medical tent "somewhat like a MASH unit." The buddy told Schwanke, "When I picked you up, you looked like my mom's sieve during raspberry time with blood coming out all over you." He was given blood transfusions and magnets were used to remove metal pieces from his face.

He lost most of the sight in his left eye and since that day it won't rotate in its socket. "I have to turn my head to see." Pieces of shrapnel too close to his spine could not be removed.

Evacuated by ship from Okinawa, Schwanke was first taken to a naval hospital in Guam and then a naval hospital in Hawaii, spending about two weeks in each place.

During the next 11 months, he was in California at the U.S. Naval Hospital, San Diego. He endured more surgeries to remove shrapnel pieces and extensive physical therapy to renew his strength. As he became stronger, hospital staff took him and other patients on outings around San Diego. He also was presented the Purple Heart while recuperating.

The war ended after Schwanke had been hospitalized for just under three months. He simply stated, "It was quite a relief."

Reflecting on his comrades who lost their lives on Okinawa, Schwanke related what he did when not in combat. "I put them in bags and attached their dog tags to the bags so they could be picked up and sent back to the U.S."

Schwanke refused a medical discharge while he was hospitalized. "I was a smart aleck and wanted to go back to active duty stateside." He stayed at Camp Pendleton and was assigned to guard duty.

His last assignment was guard duty at the Hastings (Nebraska) Naval Ammunition Depot. The War Department authorized building the $45 million structure on June 10, 1942. Hastings was chosen because of its equal distance from the Atlantic and Pacific coasts. It became the largest ammunition depot in the nation and supplied 40 percent of the Navy's ammunition during the war.

"I came home a couple of times on leave and finally got to the point where I would accept a discharge." Influencing that decision was a girlfriend back home in Nebraska, JoEllen (Joey) Green. Schwanke received his discharge on May 19, 1946.

Acknowledging that, by military standards, he is 98 percent disabled because of his hearing, vision and damage to his legs, Schwanke said he won't let pain bother him. "I can still see good out of one eye, hear out of one ear, and although my legs do hurt lots of the time, they still are attached. So, the Lord was with me." When he was dismissed from the Camp Pendleton hospital, Schwanke was told: "Get used to that wheelchair, son. You will need it full time by the time you are 50." Now, at age 90, there's no wheelchair, no walker, not even a cane.

However, there is shrapnel. In addition to the pieces by his spine, pieces remain above his left wrist. About five years after the end of the war, pieces were removed from behind his left knee. Those were saved and became part of a tie clasp. Also after the war, fabric from the pants he was wearing on June 12, 1945, was removed from his skin.

Focusing on the good memories, Schwanke stressed even though the opportunity didn't exist to form close friendships, "All the guys were absolutely like brothers and we trusted each other." Johnnie Stout, who boarded that train for boot camp with Schwanke, was a friend. "He never made it back."

Schwanke emphasized, "I was absolutely proud to serve and have no regrets about joining the Marine Corps." Another person who was proud was his father. Schwanke's parents traveled from Nebraska to see him while he was hospitalized in San Diego. "They were pleased that I still had my face and limbs."

And Schwanke's dad didn't do any hollering. "My dad was OK by then that I was a Marine."

After the war, Schwanke married Joey and the couple owned Greens Greenhouses Inc. in Fremont from 1960 until he retired in 2015. Schwanke served as national president of the Society of American Florists and was inducted into its National Hall of Fame.

Mel and Joey Schwanke live in Fremont, Nebraska, and have been married for 68 years. Their wedding date is May 12, 1948. They have 3 children, Jo, Cindy, and J; 4 grandchildren; and 6 great-grandchildren.

Charles Sharp
Marine Corps

◇◇◇◇◇◇◇◇◇◇◇◇◇◇◇◇◇◇◇◇◇◇

Birth Date:
June 29, 1923

Hometown:
Norden, Neb.

Age When Enlisted:
21

Service Dates:
July 1944 –
August 1946

Highest Rank:
Corporal

Twenty-one years old when he became a Marine, Charles Sharp, 92, referred to himself as older and a little bit wiser when he enlisted. He remembered younger comrades who were right out of high school and couldn't wait to get into combat. "Marine Corps all the way." Sharp didn't hesitate to warn those younger men, like C.J. Smith, "You know, they're going to be shooting back."

Perhaps he offered that statement because of what a drill instructor told his platoon during boot camp at Marine Corps Recruit Depot (Parris Island, South Carolina). "Don't try to be a damn hero. Try to stay alive because you ain't no good to nobody dead." That advice made an impact on Sharp. He described the instructor as an old veteran who had served overseas. "He tried to give us recruits an idea of what was coming. Of course, he told us, but it didn't sink in." However, the next sentences did sink in. "You guys are going into combat. Not all of you are coming back."

Prior to his enlistment on July 31, 1944, Sharp had been working on the family ranch in Keya Paha County, Nebraska. He had quit school in 1936 after the 8th grade. Because of his father's failing health, Sharp was needed at home. After eight years on the ranch, Sharp chose not to take a third deferment and he traveled to Kansas City to enlist. "I could join the Marine Corps, or I could go in the Army. The Marine Corps had room for five. One guy bowed out, so I was the next guy in line."

In early August, Sharp arrived at Parris Island where the recruits were formed into platoons of between 48 and 60 men. Their training schedule included learning to shoot the service rifle, pistols, the Browning Automatic Rifle (BAR) and other infantry weapons. Because rifle marksmanship was so important, more time was devoted to that skill than any other single instructional subject. Teamwork, discipline and attention to detail were continually stressed. During the war, more than 204,000 Marines received training at Parris Island.

On Dec. 3, after 2½ months at Parris Island, Sharp's platoon was sent to Camp Lejeune (Jacksonville, North Carolina) for infantry school. Sharp received training for assignment as an infantry rifleman (assistant BAR man). The base had 14 miles of beaches that made it conducive for amphibious assault training. During this time, Sharp's father died and he received leave for a couple of days to attend the funeral in Nebraska.

When he returned, his original platoon had left and Sharp was assigned to the 46th Replacement Draft on Dec. 29, 1944. Marines in a replacement draft were sent to battle areas where companies had a large number of casualties. Sharp explained men in the 46th Replacement Draft were sent to Okinawa "because they had lost so many men from the First Division."

Sharp's last move in the U.S. before leaving for the Pacific Theater took him to Camp Pendleton in San Diego County, California. At San Diego Harbor, on March 10, 1945, men in the 46th Replacement Draft boarded the USS *Arenac*. The *Arenac* was one of about 25 ships in a convoy destined for Guam. The ship stopped in Hawaii (Pearl Harbor), crossed the International Date Line on March 24, stopped in the Marshall Islands and arrived in Guam on April 1. Also on April 1, 1945, the 1st Marine Division, nicknamed Old Breed, landed with the 6th Marine Division on the northern Hagushi beaches of Okinawa. Five divisions of the 10th Army also were landing on the island. By nightfall, 60,000 American troops were ashore. Seizing control of Okinawa was key for the U.S. military as the island could be used as a support base for a scheduled November invasion of Japan proper.

Just over five weeks later, on May 11, Marines in the 46th Replacement Draft left on the USS *Dickens* for Okinawa. They arrived on May 15. Sharp said mopping up was

157

the main job for the Marines in the 46th Replacement Draft. Mopping up was completing a military campaign by killing or capturing any remaining enemy troops. "Our mission was to direct all the Japs down to one end of the island so we could make them surrender." Sharp added that about half of the island had been secured before the 46th Replacement Draft arrived. "All the real tough battles had been fought." But Sharp and other Marines in the 46th Replacement Draft still had battles of their own. "We would run into these ambushes. And, of course, the snipers were bad."

A rifle squad of four Marines was called a fire team. Each fire team was composed of a BAR man, a BAR assistant, a scout and a team leader. Their positions in combat followed the shape of a diamond. Up front was the scout, a marksman armed with an M1903 Springfield (standard issue infantry rifle) with a rifle grenade discharger. Below and to the left was the BAR man. Directly across from the BAR man was the assistant BAR man. And straight down from the scout was the fire team leader armed with an M1 carbine or M1 SMG (submachine gun).

As the assistant BAR man, Sharp was responsible for carrying 12 magazines, each consisting of 20 rounds. The BAR man carried the rifle and 13 magazines, 12 in his ammunition belt and one in the BAR. The Browning Automatic Rifle was air-cooled, gas-operated and could fire 120-150 rounds per minute. Its maximum effective range was 600 yards.

Ammunition, water and food for the men on Okinawa were dropped with parachutes from airplanes. "Of course, it was out in the open and it was pretty tough going to get it because the Japs were there."

Most evenings just before dark, the Marines dug foxholes as places to sleep and to provide protection from enemy fire. "Those foxholes were pretty close together. Two guys in a foxhole." Sharp had a preference with whom he wanted to share a foxhole. "The guys I wanted to be in a foxhole with were the old boys from West Virginia. They were tough and they could shoot, too."

One evening after digging a foxhole, he admitted, "We were getting ready to settle in for the night and I don't know what I was thinking." Sharp decided he wanted to see a buddy who was maybe four foxholes away from him. "I left everything in the foxhole. My rifle. I didn't even wear my helmet. I looked down in a foxhole. There was an old boy and he had his rifle pointed right straight at my head. I don't know why he didn't shoot me. I got my butt back in my foxhole and I stayed there. That's when you know the good Lord is watching out for you."

The Marines kept moving forward toward Dakeshi Ridge. That's where, Sharp noted, the Japanese had their last stronghold. "We figured we would get them corralled there and then we could force them to surrender." Sharp said men of the 46th Replacement Draft stayed around Dakeshi Ridge for a couple of days. During that time a reconnaissance patrol was in the front lines and got pinned down. The purpose of a reconnaissance patrol was to obtain information about the position and activities of the Japanese. One Marine was wounded. Sharp explained because he and Schaefer (the BAR man) "had the only firepower," they were sent with the stretcher-bearers to rescue the injured man. They followed the edge of the seawall and then walked along a small creek to where they found the injured Marine. Once he was transferred to the stretcher, the men tried to stay out of sight by walking through weeds. "They couldn't see us, but they kept firing at us. We were really lucky. Nobody got hit."

Once the Marines got back to the seawall, Sharp said they were running in knee-deep water. Both Sharp and Schaefer fell and suffered knee injuries. "Them damn coral rocks. We were in pretty bad shape when we came in and they took us to sick bay." It was nightfall on May 12, while Sharp and Schaefer were in sick bay, that the Marines and Army men captured Dakeshi Ridge.

By the end of the 82-day campaign in Okinawa, more than 12,000 American servicemen were killed and more than 83,000 were wounded or missing. Just a little over six weeks after the Battle of Okinawa ended (June 22, 1945), the atomic bomb was dropped on Hiroshima (Aug. 6, 1945). "We really didn't believe it that the war was over. That's when we loaded up and we thought we were going home."

But, Sharp did not go home. On Sept. 26, 1945, the men in the 46th Replacement Draft left Okinawa aboard the USS *Randall* and arrived in Taku, China. Sharp said he found out they were going to China when "that's where we landed." Called Operation Beleaguer, this was a major U.S. military operation. The main objectives were the repatriation of more than 600,000 Japanese and Koreans and the protection of Americans. "The worst part about going to China was we got ahead of our food. We didn't have any food. But we'd been in combat and we could scrounge, so we didn't have to worry about that."

After the Marines arrived, the Chinese had a parade. "There were like a million people. They were thanking us and sure were glad to see us. One old veteran said, 'They're excited to see us come and they'll be a sight damn gladder to see us leave.' And that was probably right." During his time in China, Sharp rode coal trains across the country to provide protection against Communist sabotaging. He later served as a jeep driver for the officer-of-the-day. He was stationed for about 10 months in northern China (Tientsin and Tong Shan). Aboard the USS *General H.W. Butner*, Sharp left Taku on July 25, 1946. It arrived in San Diego on Aug. 9 and Sharp was discharged there on Aug. 21, 1946.

After 25 months in the Marine Corps, Sharp could again consider himself older and a little bit wiser than when he enlisted. He witnessed firsthand what that drill sergeant had said. "Not all of you are coming back."

Sharp's own words sunk in for C.J. Smith. "You know, they're going to be shooting back." It was just about three weeks after Sharp's comment to the young Marine when they saw each other again. "He'd been through some tough times. He said, 'Sharp, you were sure right.' That's the only thing he said."

◇◇◇◇◇◇◇◇◇◇◇◇◇◇◇◇◇◇◇◇

After the war, Sharp was a rancher in Valentine and Obert, both in Nebraska, and Milboro, South Dakota. He worked for the State of Nebraska Game and Parks Commission (Valentine Fish Hatchery and Ponca State Park). In 2003, Sharp retired as a veterinarian assistant for Michael Foods in Wakefield, Nebraska.

Charles and JoAnn Sharp live in Wakefield, Nebraska, and have been married for 67 years. Their wedding date is June 1, 1949. They have 5 children, Charliss, Corliss, Nancy, Jim, and Jeremy; 11 grandchildren; and 11 great-grandchildren.

WATCH THE GAP

See www.mta.info for Fare & Ticket Information

331398094

Valid thru:08/24/17

Metro-North Railroad

1	2	3	4	5	6	7

HARRISN 13
NEW ROC 12

One Ride in either direction.
Refundable within 60 days from date of purchase.
Subject to $10 refund fee per transaction.

OW Intermediate

Subject to applicable tariff regulations and conditions of use. See www.mta.info.

0
577
17:44

675115
06/26/17
331398094

Credit $3.00 4603

Laddie Socha
Army

◇◇◇◇◇◇◇◇◇◇◇◇◇◇◇◇◇◇◇◇◇◇◇◇

Birth Date:
Oct. 12, 1924

Hometown:
Primrose, Neb.

Age When Enlisted:
18

Service Dates:
July 1943 –
December 1945

Highest Rank:
Private First Class

Enlisting in the military before being drafted could result in a first choice selection for preferred service branch. For Laddie Socha, 92, that didn't happen. In fact, he didn't get his first choice or his second choice. He turned down the third option and that left the Army.

At age 18 in July 1943, Socha traveled 157 miles from his hometown of Primrose, Nebraska, to Fort Crook (now Offutt Air Force Base) outside of Omaha, Nebraska. "After I had signed in, they asked which branch of the service I would like to be in." He replied Air Force [Army Air Forces]. "Well, they said the Air Force quota is full. What's next?" Socha replied Navy. "That quota is full. Marines?" He didn't want the Marines. "So that left me in the Army with no other choice."

Because Socha was still in high school and because there were already two Socha brothers in the service, he received a deferment to finish high school. "Before I graduated in May, I went to the draft board because I knew I was going to be drafted one way or the other. I would have been a 1A." The 1A classification meant a man was available and fit for general military service.

In addition to Socha, brothers Joe (Army), Rudy (Army) and Gene (Navy) served during World War II. Oldest brother Emil wasn't drafted because he was married and had a child. Jim was in the Air Force during the Korean War.

Just like enlisting in the military did not guarantee Socha would be accepted for the Army Air Forces, excelling as a marksman during six weeks of basic training at Fort Leonard Wood, Missouri, did not result in an Army infantry assignment. Expert is the top qualification in the Army marksmanship training course and out of 40 targets, hitting 36-40 targets is required. Referring to his expert shooting, Socha said, "Of course, us country boys knew how to shoot better than the city boys."

But, Army officials wanted someone who could do more than shoot a gun. "When they found out I could type, I became a clerk and was on duty seven days a week. The good Lord must have been looking after me." At one time, Socha was handling personnel records for about 800 soldiers in one battalion. "I was confined pretty much to what was going on in the company and battalion. Didn't have to know everything."

Before Socha kept soldiers' files updated, he had orders to attend camouflage school at Fort Belvoir in Virginia. "That was the first time that I had ever seen mixing water with something to make paint and I had to learn how to camouflage netting." Given a couple of needles, Socha was shown how to sew the fishnet-like material into 2-inch squares for a final dimension about 40 feet by 40 feet. He learned how to combine paints for camouflage colors to be used on jeeps and tanks. Finally, strips of brown, orange and green cloth were woven through the netting. "The netting was designed to cover trucks and tanks so it looked like dirt from the air."

Just short of six months after he enlisted, Socha left New York City on Jan. 1, 1944, for an overseas assignment. "We were supposed to go directly to Southampton, England, but the scuttlebutt was there was a pack of German submarines after our ship." He said the first couple of days "was like a vacation" because the water was smooth, the sun was shining and everybody was sitting on the deck. The third day had everyone wearing coats because the ship had headed toward Iceland and Greenland. "We ended up at Glasgow, Scotland, because of the German submarines."

From Scotland, Socha boarded a train for Birmingham, England, where he waited about six weeks for his unit assignment. His orders were to join an engineer outfit at Land's End, England. "That's that little bitty tail point clear down in England." From February until June 10, 1944, his unit was training with other units on beaches simulated for landing in France on Utah Beach (Normandy).

On June 6, Allied forces had landed at Utah Beach. Socha explained even though his unit was with the forces that initially hit Utah Beach, he didn't arrive until four days later. That's because his company was the rear echelon, located at a distance from the front and focused mainly on administrative and supply duties. "I was always in combat zones but never in combat. When I came in, the beaches were all cleared. There were a few tanks that had been knocked out [at Utah Beach] and I could see a few German bodies still lying there."

Staying on Utah Beach for about four months, Socha said his "office" was in a pillbox with the colonel. Pillboxes were concrete dug-in guard posts, often camouflaged and normally built with openings for firing weapons. The name was derived from the perceived similarity to boxes that held medical pills.

What was the assignment on Utah Beach? "Not doing much of anything. Don't know why we were there that long. Just did our job and that was it." His job involved getting orders from the company commander. "I didn't get to know everything that was going on. I did what the company commander said to do. There was no set daily routine. Every day was different."

And, one day, something happened on Utah Beach that wasn't routine. "I'll never forget it. It was a Sunday and we were sitting outside our pup tents and writing letters home." The man sitting next to Socha looked down and saw something shiny. Wondering what it was, the two men began pushing sand away from the object. "It was a tank mine and we were sitting within 2 to 3 feet of the danged thing. We called the captain and he sent a couple of guys who were trained using mine detectors." Socha said the "doggone thing was full of sand" when it was dug up. "Here we had been sitting and the trucks had been driving over the cotton-pickin' thing and it never did go off." The mine was defused and dumped in the ocean. "So they did sweep that whole area and that was the only mine they found." Admitting the live tank mine created a tense moment, Socha said there was no other time he felt threatened or in danger. "I was one of the more fortunate ones."

Because of frequent position movements, Socha said there were lots of individually packaged C-ration meals. "It was supposed to be nutritious, but I don't know how people survived because a lot of guys wouldn't even eat the stuff." Describing what was included in a C-ration meal, he said there were scrambled eggs (water was not added), ground meat, cheese, sometimes a chocolate bar and a piece of chewing gum, cigarettes and a biscuit so hard "you could hardly chew it." He added: "There were lots of the same thing. We grumbled, but we survived. And to this day I will not eat Spam because I had my fill of it."

When Socha's unit spent longer periods of time at a base camp, a cook was on duty. "We didn't get T-bone steak or anything like that, but the meals were pretty decent." Still, Socha missed his mother's cooking, especially her kolaches. In packages sent from home, he never received mom's kolaches but he did receive her cookies.

The unit moved a lot, so "sometimes we wouldn't get mail for two or three months. Mail call was always important." All letters Socha sent home were censored, and he couldn't let his parents know specifically where he was. He wanted to keep a personal journal because of a gift from his high school classmates. The cover of the 4½"x6" black book reads, *My Life in the Service.* Nicely written on the first page is, "Presented by The Class of 1944, Primrose High School at the Junior-Senior Banquet as a token of appreciation for your service to our country." However, men were told not to keep journals in case they got into German hands. Nothing could be written that gave specific locations. "I did take the diary with me, thinking I could write in it, but I never put a word in it. I've got a lot of names of the guys who I was in the service with stuck in that book, but that's about all."

As battalion clerk, Socha also picked up and distributed mail. While stationed in Aachen, Germany, he drove about 40 miles from Aachen to Brussels, Belgium, for mail pickup. The round trip took about an hour. Returning from Brussels on May 7, 1945, he saw the entire company standing outside the main office. "I thought, 'What in the world is going on? They're supposed to be working.'" Then he was told, "The war is over!" It was May 7 when Germany officially surrendered to the Allies.

Socha described how everybody was hollering and screaming, but after things settled down, they had to get back to work. He stayed and served as clerk until July when he became eligible for discharge. "I was in Belgium the day the Japanese surrendered in August [15th]." Some younger men also waiting to board a ship for home were ready to celebrate. They were mixing orange pop and vodka. "I said, 'Well, I'll drink one or two.' Well, one or two led to a few more and a few more." The amount of vodka added to the orange pop was light, Socha said. "We could just sit there and drink and drink and not know how much we were drinking. It tasted just like orange pop but with quite a kick."

After the ship Socha was aboard arrived in New York City on Dec. 16, 1945, his next destination was Fort Leavenworth, Kansas, to officially receive his discharge on Dec. 31, 1945. "They sent me on a bus from Fort Leavenworth to Omaha and then I got a train to Columbus and then Primrose."

His parents did not know he was coming home. Even if he had written a letter, the Army clerk who delivered mail stated, "I would have beaten it home." More important than mail arriving home was that brothers Joe, Rudy and Gene also made it home.

After the war, Socha worked for different farmers for about three years before going to Oregon to look for a job. He returned to Nebraska and worked at the Armour Packing Plant in Omaha. For eight years, Socha was in sales at the T.B. Hord Grain and Lumber Company in Primrose, Nebraska. His final job before retirement in 1990 was at S&S Lumber Company in Norfolk, Nebraska, for 26 years. Socha moved to Fremont, Nebraska, in 1995.

Laddie Socha lives in Fremont, Nebraska, and was married to Helen for 63 years. Their wedding date is April 10, 1950. They have 4 children, Pamela, Jackie, Keith, and Daryl; 6 grandchildren; and 12 great-grandchildren.

Marvin Welstead
Army Air Corps

◇◇◇◇◇◇◇◇◇◇◇◇◇◇◇◇◇◇◇◇◇◇◇

Birth Date:
Feb. 21, 1921

Hometown:
Fremont, Neb.

Age When Drafted:
21

Service Dates:
September 1942 –
December 1945

Highest Rank:
Sergeant

"What in the hell are you doing here?" Probably not the question from a doctor that a sergeant is expecting to hear at a medical exam prior to discharge on Dec. 20, 1945. That's exactly what Marv Welstead, 95, heard before he answered, "Now's a fine time to tell me."

That was the third time Welstead had heard a similar question during his 39 months in the service, just phrased differently. "When I was drafted and went for my physical, apparently they found a heart murmur." He was hospitalized for three days at Fort Crook (12 miles south of Omaha, Nebraska). After release from the hospital, he was sworn in for service with the Army Air Corps on Sept. 26, 1942. He arrived at Fort Leavenworth in Kansas on Oct. 6. Another exam. "After my physical, they put me in the hospital again for a couple of days. The heart murmur had been detected again. They had to decide if they were going to send me on or not."

The decision was not to send him home and instead he proceeded to Stuttgart Army Airfield in Arkansas on Oct. 9, 1942. He would be attending advanced flying school. What was missing before he went to Stuttgart was basic training. "I'm 95 years old and I haven't had my basic training yet." After he missed basic training, something else was missing when Welstead, 14 other men and a first lieutenant arrived at Stuttgart. No one was at the train station to meet them. And then the station attendant said: "You are among the first. They are just building that base."

The station attendant told the men they could find a colonel on the second floor above the drugstore downtown. "So 15 guys who had been in the service about six or eight days were walking down the streets of this town." When they arrived at the base, there were no buildings. Assuring the men he would find them beds, the colonel said there were tarpaper shacks on concrete blocks that would be used as their barracks. Welstead said the shacks were in a former rice field. "So, my first assignment in the service was building wooden sidewalks around where the barracks were."

From the opening of Stuttgart Army Airfield in October 1942, Welstead saw the facility grow from only the tarpaper shacks and the wooden sidewalks to eventually have four 5,000-foot runways and 6,000 personnel. Seven aux-iliary fields also were constructed. Initially, the Army Air Forces Training Command used the facility as a glider pilot training school until May 1943. That same month and year, the airfield was transferred to Southeast Training Command and pilots began attending twin-engine flying school. After those pilots completed training at Stuttgart, they attended school elsewhere for learning to fly the B-17 and B-25 bombers. The twin-engine training ceased in January 1945 when the airfield was transferred to the Third Air Force.

While Welstead was waiting for a permanent assign-ment, the first lieutenant looked through the men's files. In Fremont, Nebraska, before he was drafted, Welstead worked in positions of inventory control for J.C. Penney and Montgomery Ward. Noting his work experience, Wel-stead said the first lieutenant told him, "We want you to be chief clerk of ordnance." That position primarily involved handling supplies, and Welstead immediately began order-ing jeeps and trucks. They were shipped to ports of embar-kation and loaded onto troop ships destined for overseas.

The first lieutenant asked Welstead, who had only been at Stuttgart for three weeks, another question. "Is your wife a stenographer?" On his 21st birthday (Feb. 21, 1942), Welstead had married his high school sweetheart, Jean Olson. Telling the officer yes in response to the ques-tion, the officer continued: "Headquarters says we need a stenographer. Send for her." When she arrived at Stuttgart on Nov. 22, it was Jean Welstead's 20th birthday.

"I tell people that Jean and I served together." Always a civilian, Jean was responsible for keeping accurate records on all planes flying in and out of Stuttgart. "She had 3"x5" cards and set up the planes by their numbers. She recorded who landed at what time from what base and flying back to what base." For just over a month, Welstead continued his responsibilities as chief clerk and Jean hers as stenographer. Then a master sergeant arrived and assumed the chief clerk position and Welstead was reassigned as assistant clerk.

Another assignment came at the end of January 1943 when Welstead got orders to relocate to California and enroll in business classes at Woodbury College. The Welsteads arrived in Los Angeles and reported to the Willard Hotel. "I told the sergeant that I'd like to get Jean settled and we went to the YMCA." An employee there informed the Welsteads: "I have a nice place for you. I think I can get you a room in Pickfair."

This "nice place" was a 4-story, 25-room mansion owned by silent-film actors Douglas Fairbanks and Mary Pickford. They were not living in the mansion at the time and their decision was "to take in soldiers." Welstead was able to stay at Pickfair with Jean except for one requirement. The sergeant told Welstead: "You are to bunk here at the hotel. But if your wife is here, I don't care when you come and go just so you are in bed here at 11 o'clock at night and up for reveille [wake-up call] at 7 o'clock in the morning."

At Pickfair, the Welsteads had a large room right by the front door. "Of all things, it had a built-in bar. We put a hot plate there." His rent check (from a housing allowance) was written to Douglas Fairbanks. "Pickfair was a beautiful house."

Attending Ordnance Clerical School, in addition to business classes at Woodbury College, Welstead also took English and math classes that civilian professors taught. "Then at 4 o'clock in the afternoon, we'd meet with our Army captain and Army major and we talked about procurement and finances — Army style." After completing eight weeks of classes, the Welsteads left Pickfair and California on May 31, 1943, for a two-week furlough in Fremont. Their next stop was back at Stuttgart Army Airfield. Since the master sergeant who had assumed the chief clerk position was still there, Welstead worked in the parts department for about three months.

Then the master sergeant was relocated and Welstead once again became chief clerk (2nd Tactical Command, 3rd Air Force). He supervised the activities of nine warehouse men and eight civilian female clerks. Welstead recalled having about 1,200 trucks and jeeps in his inventory. The base population eventually grew to about 20,000.

Upon her return to Stuttgart, Jean began working in the Rail Transportation Department. "When the cadets finished their training, she typed up the routing for troop trains to take these guys wherever they were to go."

After the bombing of Pearl Harbor on Dec. 7, 1941, and the entrance of the United States into World War II, consumer goods took a back seat to military production.

In May 1942, the U.S. Office of Price Administration froze prices on most goods used daily in American households. This resulted in war ration books and tokens being issued to American families. Across the country, 8,000 rationing boards were created to administer the restrictions on items including sugar, coffee, gasoline and tires.

The lieutenant colonel at Stuttgart was responsible for naming a Post Ration Officer for the base and he chose Jean. Everyone on base had to see Jean for their stamps, Welstead said. "I used to tease Jean because she had the authority to call for the colonel's staff car and driver. Then she would go to the ration meetings in Stuttgart [about seven miles from the airfield] at the County Ration Board and pick up her groceries."

The Welsteads stayed at Stuttgart in their own apartment on the base as they continued their respective jobs — he as chief clerk and she in Rail Transportation — for about the next 15 months (September 1944 to December 1945). However, in August 1945, Welstead said it was decided "that all of us had to qualify for overseas." While on an obstacle course, he passed out because of his heart murmur and was hospitalized. "While I was in the hospital, I heard the war was over."

After he was released from the hospital, Welstead "went right back to my desk" until his orders came through to be discharged. "We had been closing the base down until there was probably about 200 of us left. I would type up the orders to ship out the jeeps and the trucks." He explained trains arrived with flat cars. "Our guys would put these jeeps and trucks on these flat cars and anchor them down. Jean and I would walk the tracks at night to check them all to make sure they were all anchored down." Many of the vehicles were directed to the Red River Ordnance Depot in Texas, west of Texarkana, where they were stored.

Welstead learned on Dec. 15 that he was being discharged. "I went to Jean and she typed up my tickets home. When she finished, she turned to the warrant officer and said, 'I quit.' He responded, 'I wonder why.'"

The Scott Field separation center, 25 miles east of St. Louis, Missouri, was where Welstead heard the doctor say, "What in the hell are you doing here?" Hospitalized again for three days because of his heart murmur, Welstead noted: "The doctor said, 'I'll go ahead and discharge you. You report to the Vet's Hospital on Jan. 5 in Omaha.'" It was Dec. 20, 1945.

After the Welsteads were back in Fremont, he kept the Jan. 5 appointment. "I went there and sat from 8 in the morning until 3 in the afternoon. Finally, someone took my blood pressure and said, 'The doctor will see you in two weeks.'" In two weeks, Welstead drove for the second time to the Veterans Hospital in Omaha. "On Jan. 19, I go back and the same thing happened. Sat there all day, took my blood pressure at 3 o'clock. 'The doctor will see you in two weeks.' I never went back."

Never went back? "Never did. I haven't been there since Jan. 19, 1946. I'm AWOL from there to this day."

◇◇◇◇◇◇◇◇◇◇◇◇◇◇◇◇◇◇◇◇◇◇◇◇

After the war, Welstead worked at Equitable Federal Savings Bank in Fremont. He began working with GI loans and retired as president in 1984. He then worked for the Federal Deposit Insurance Corporation (FDIC) from 1989-92.

Marv Welstead lives in Fremont, Nebraska, and was married to Jean for 67 years. Their wedding date is Feb. 21, 1942. They have 2 sons, Bob and Jon; 3 grandchildren; and 3 great-grandchildren.

Bob Wiegand
Merchant Marine

◇◇◇◇◇◇◇◇◇◇◇◇◇◇◇◇◇◇◇◇

Birth Date:
Sept. 23, 1925

Hometown:
Cedar Bluffs, Neb.

Age When Enlisted:
18

Service Dates:
November 1944 –
January 1946

Highest Rank:
Fireman/Watertender

After serving on cargo ships in the South Pacific, Bob Wiegand, 91, returned to his home in Cedar Bluffs, Nebraska. Because he served as a Merchant Marine, he received no government benefits, could not take advantage of the GI Bill to help continue his education at the University of Nebraska and did not have veteran status.

"I was pretty burned up about that. I might have finished college. In those days, we didn't have any money and sure didn't make any money in the service. I was 18-years-old and got a letter from Uncle Sam that you have been selected to serve in the service." That letter began a 42-year wait for Wiegand to be recognized as a U.S. military veteran.

When he reported to Fort Riley (Kansas) in November 1944, Wiegand was ready to enlist in the Navy. He was told there wasn't a need for Navy recruits. He was sent home and had 10 days to decide if he wanted to enlist in the Army. He also was told, "We need people in the Merchant Marine." Wiegand grew up on a farm and said he didn't know the Merchant Marine "from a bale of hay." With his decision made to join the Merchant Marine, Wiegand returned after the 10 days and reported to a recruiting station in Kansas City. During his service from Nov. 20, 1944, until Jan. 31, 1946, Wiegand would learn that the Merchant Marine transported supplies, equipment and troops for the war effort.

His first destination was Catalina Island, 22 miles off California, for boot camp. Aboard a cruise ship to reach the island, it was the first time Wiegand had seen the Pacific Ocean. "I was a Nebraskan, so the Platte River was about it for me."

Training on the island for about a month, 30-35 men were taken to towers that were 70-75 feet high. Before jumping off a tower, Wiegand explained, "They taught us the fundamentals of a life jacket and how to handle it if we had to jump off a ship." The life jacket was held down so it wouldn't come open or "you could break your neck."

After a month at Catalina Island, Wiegand was sent to San Francisco. He emphasized that was where the association with the U.S. military ended and the connection with the private sector began. Once in San Francisco, Wiegand had to sign up with the union. During World War II,

American President Lines served as an agent for the War Shipping Administration and oversaw the administration of hundreds of vessels.

Wiegand was first assigned to the SS *Isaac I. Stevens*. For six months, he was aboard that Liberty ship. Named after prominent deceased Americans, Liberty ships had been introduced in 1941 and could be mass-produced cheaply and quickly using assembly-line methods. Isaac Ingalls Stevens was a brigadier general in the union Army during the Civil War. Each Liberty ship carried a crew of 38-62 civilian merchant sailors and 21-40 Navy personnel to operate defensive guns and communications equipment. According to American Merchant Marine at War (www.usmm.org), a Liberty ship was 441 feet long and 56 feet wide. Her three-cylinder, reciprocating steam engine was fed by two oil-burning boilers. Her five holds could carry over 9,000 tons of cargo, plus airplanes, tanks and locomotives lashed to its deck. A Liberty ship could carry 2,840 jeeps, 440 tanks or 230 million rounds of rifle ammunition.

The *Isaac I. Stevens* was a cargo ship loaded with ammunition and Wiegand was assigned as a Wiper. "That was the bottom." As a rookie, he worked with others who had experience with boilers. "I was with a Fireman/Water-tender, which is the next step above Wiper. He taught me the ropes." What was the job of a Wiper? "Doing whatever you're told." Wiegand clarified that he worked in the engine room and cleaned the boilers and reciprocating engine. The boilers created the steam that operated the engine. The reciprocating engine is also known as an internal-combustion engine.

Outside San Francisco, the ship became part of a convoy that Wiegand estimated probably included 50-60 other ships. Battleships, cruisers and many destroyers were traveling with the *Isaac I. Stevens*. "The destroyers kept circling all the time." Traveling in a zigzag route to confuse Japanese submarines, the convoy ships moved at 9 or 10 knots. One knot equals 1.15 miles per hour.

Luzon, the largest island in the Philippines and location of Manila, was the destination for the *Isaac I. Stevens*. Much of the ammunition it was carrying would be unloaded on Luzon. One week before the ship's arrival, General Douglas McArthur successfully directed the invasion of Luzon. More than 60,000 American troops landed on the island on Jan. 9, 1945. By Aug. 15, the Japanese lost the battle for Luzon and eventually control over all the Philippines. Wiegand said he "could see them fighting up there in the hills." He also saw young native children paddle small boats to the ships anchored in Lingayen Gulf. "They were trying to sell their woven baskets. Here are the guys on the island fighting. It just didn't make sense to me."

Cargo ships usually had several engines for different uses. Main, or propulsion engines that burned heavy fuel oil, were used to turn the ship's propeller and move the ship through the ocean. Water was brought to a boil in the boiler room and then the steam was transmitted directly to the large reciprocating engine, where it was utilized to power the ship. Wiegand said it was pretty hot in the engine room that was "as large as a small house." Located in the middle of the ship, there were large ventilators and if he stood under them, "There was a pretty good breeze."

When the *Isaac I. Stevens* left the Philippines, it dropped off medical supplies in New Guinea. Then, after six months on the water, Wiegand said the ship returned to San Francisco and he was discharged from the ship on May 23, 1945.

Granted a month of leave, Wiegand bought a train ticket and returned to Cedar Bluffs. For the second of four times, he was on a train that stopped at the North Platte Canteen in western Nebraska. The troops didn't get off the train, but the girls and women walked beside the cars. "They brought out bushel baskets of fruit and cookies. It was great. I'd never seen anything like that."

Reporting back to San Francisco, Wiegand and a buddy, Loyd Sukstorf from Cedar Bluffs, were assigned to the same ship, *MacMurray Victory*. Another cargo Liberty ship, it was newly built by Kaiser Shipyards. With four shipyards in the San Francisco Bay area, Kaiser was the largest shipbuilding operation on the Pacific Coast. In 1936, President Roosevelt appointed five men to the U.S. Maritime Commission that directed the country's shipbuilding program. The Liberty ship and the Victory ship, on which Wiegand served, were privately — not government — owned.

On July 6, 1945, Wiegand boarded the *MacMurray Victory* with a promotion because of his time served and experience. His assignment was still in the boiler/engine room, but his rank was Fireman/Watertender. He was one of three Firemen responsible for keeping the boilers running and clean. As Watertender, he turned valves to maintain water levels. Fresh water was loaded in San Francisco and the ship never had to load more.

The ship stopped to load cargo at Port Hueneme Sea-Bee Base, which is 60 miles northwest of Los Angeles. The word Seabee is derived from the initials "CB" for Construction Battalion. A Seabee is a member of the United States Naval Construction Forces. "We even carried an airbase with us." That meant loading mats as big as a room in a house, which were used for runways. The cargo ships had five holds and each hold had a crane to lift the mats and other equipment necessary for outfitting an air base. The Seabees were responsible for building airbases, including placing mats that were carried on cargo ships to make airstrips. To help with construction, the Seabees used a lot of dynamite. Packed in burlap-type bags, Wiegand estimated each bag held about 80 pounds of powdered dynamite. "Our number one hold was full of dynamite — 10,000 tons or better." The cargo holds were metal and the walls were lined with wood.

Leaving Port Hueneme, the *MacMurray Victory* joined another convoy and headed straight for Okinawa. When the convoy arrived at Buckner Bay, the Battle of Okinawa had ended less than a month earlier. Fighting took place from April 1 until June 22, 1945, and was the largest amphibious landing in the Pacific Theater.

Wiegand and the *MacMurray Victory* may have missed the Battle of Okinawa but were in the direct path of the Makurazaki Typhoon. "I will never forget the date of Sept. 17, 1945." He said nothing, including the 10,000 tons of dynamite, had been unloaded from the ship that was anchored in Buckner Bay. The extra weight helped keep the ship upright. "We were carrying a full load, including all kinds of construction supplies, Army trucks and jeeps on the decks. The ship was anchored. A lot of smaller ships like mine sweepers would get washed ashore." If the ships were not loaded, "The sterns would come up and the crews couldn't throttle them down and the ships would go sideways with the waves and just roll."

He estimated waves from the typhoon reached a height of 70-80 feet and water ran down the ship's smokestack. He described the scene: "We had both anchors down. We had our engines going slow speed ahead. One anchor broke. And if you've ever seen an anchor on these ships, they're big. The links are big around. One broke and then the other one broke. The captain put the ship in full speed ahead right smack into the storm. The floating dry dock that was right next to us broke loose and hit us. It put a big dent in the side but luckily it was above the water level, so we didn't take any water on. But it sure put a dent in that new ship."

During storms, the men were expected to remain at their stations. Once, Wiegand said the other two Firemen were seasick and he had to stay on duty for nearly 30 hours to keep the boilers going.

In October or November 1945, the *MacMurray Victory* headed for Wilmington, California, where Wiegand was discharged on Jan. 3, 1946. The route included a stop at Pearl Harbor. "Before they let us come into Pearl Harbor, we had to dump overboard all that dynamite in the number one hold. You'd be surprised what's out there in the ocean."

Back in California, he was again discharged from the ship. He had made the rank of Oiler but never served in that capacity because he was never on another ship.

Forty-four years after his service with the Merchant Marine ended, Wiegand received a letter dated Sept. 28, 1989. Signed by Captain F.J. Grady, U.S. Coast Guard, it stated: "The valuable and often valiant service of the American Merchant Marine has long been recognized. That service has now been recognized as having veterans status. Please accept the enclosed Certificate of Release or Discharge From Active Duty and Honorable Discharge Certificate presented on behalf of a grateful nation." Another sentence in the letter quoted a grateful General Douglas MacArthur and perhaps eased a little of Wiegand's resentment. "I hold no branch in higher esteem than the Merchant Marine Services."

More lasting than a letter on faded stationery is a permanent reminder of Wiegand's "valuable service" — a tattoo on his right arm just below his elbow. On Margaret Street in San Francisco, December 1944, he had selected an anchor with U.S.M.M. (United States Merchant Marine) printed on it.

◇◇◇◇◇◇◇◇◇◇◇◇◇◇◇◇◇◇

After the war, Wiegand went home to Cedar Bluffs, Nebraska, and farmed with his family. He married in 1949, and he and Donna had their own place near Cedar Bluffs. They farmed (with dairy cattle) until 1964. For 10 years, Wiegand worked for the Fremont (Nebraska) Farmers Union and left as assistant manager. He was hired as manager of the Farmers Union Coop in Mead, Nebraska, retiring in 1985. Wiegand then drove a bus for the Cedar Bluffs Public Schools for 20 years.

Donna and Bob Wiegand live in Cedar Bluffs, Nebraska, and have been married for 67 years. Their wedding date is Sept. 11, 1949. They have 2 daughters, Deb and Becky; 2 grandchildren; and 4 great-grandchildren.

ACKNOWLEDGMENTS

I am Forever Grateful to:

My veterans and their family members, who will remain a very special part of my life. They shared time, pictures, documents and, most importantly, memories.

◇◇◇◇◇◇◇◇◇◇◇◇◇◇◇◇◇◇◇◇

Nancy Wagner, who is a published author and handled the publication process through Prairieland Press. I have said more than once that she could publish this book without me, but I could not publish the book without her.

◇◇◇◇◇◇◇◇◇◇◇◇◇◇◇◇◇◇◇◇

Lynn Gibney, who designed the cover and inside-page layout. She professionally applied on paper what I sometimes could not see in my head.

◇◇◇◇◇◇◇◇◇◇◇◇◇◇◇◇◇◇◇◇

Marilyn Peterson, who taught my first collegiate Journalism class that resulted in me becoming a Journalism major. She gave me her collection of World War II memorabilia and offered the advice, "Know when to stop tweaking."

Gary Overfield, who is a retired high school English teacher. He was the perfect choice for my content reader and had the opportunity to continue honing his expertise on comma placement.

Dean Jacobs, who is a world traveler and awesome photographer. He took the current pictures of my veterans when he wasn't off in some other part of the world.

Sue Bristol, Cheryl Paden, Janet Todd and Nancy Wagner, who are members of My Thoughts Exactly writers' group. They offered suggestions and encouragement during all phases of the book.

Doug Winfield, who kept our household functioning while I spent hours interviewing, researching, writing and revising. His support was unwavering; without my husband, *Forever Heroes* would never have been finished.

ABOUT THE AUTHOR

Dr. Joyce H. Winfield was a high school teacher (Journalism) and college professor (Journalism and English) for 22 years before leaving academia. She earned her Ph.D. in Mass Communication from the University of Minnesota and her M.A. in Mass Communication from the University of Nebraska at Omaha.

Writing Resources, the business she started in 2008, provides her the opportunity to continue working with words through writing, editing and proofreading.

Her father planned yearly summer vacations. Before she graduated from high school, she had traveled in all states but Hawaii. Those vacations included stops at historical sites, which instilled an early love for the past.

The combination of the joy of writing and the fascination of history culminated in *Forever Heroes*.

Winfield lives in Fremont, Nebraska, with Doug, her husband, and Jesse, their toy poodle.

43761315R00120

Made in the USA
Middletown, DE
18 May 2017